CAUTION:
SOUL MATE AHEAD!

Spiritual Love in the Physical World

Janet Cunningham, Ph.D.
Michael Ranucci

Second Edition 1999

Published in the United States by:
Two Suns Press
Post Office Box 55
Columbia, Maryland 21045-0055
USA

Copyright © by Janet Cunningham, Ph.D. and Michael Ranucci
All rights reserved.
No part of this book may be reproduced or utilized in any form
without permission in writing from the authors.

Poetry and illustrations: Michael Ranucci
Cover art: Spirit Creative Services, Inc., Alice Yeager, Illustrator
Original cover design: David W. Howell
Copyediting: Joanne Garland

Library of Congress No. 94-090007

ISBN 0-9640026-9-8

Other books by Janet Cunningham, Ph.D.

A Tribe Returned

Inner Selves: The Feminine* Path to Weight Loss
(*for men and women who value their intuitive nature.)

Other poetry by Michael Ranucci

Expressions of Running Deer

Aquarelle

For information about Seminars and private counseling
with Janet Cunningham, Ph.D. and/or
Michael Ranucci:

http://www.JanetCunningham.com

DEDICATION

This book is dedicated
with deep love and appreciation
to our greatest teachers
—our Soul Mates.

ACKNOWLEDGMENTS

It is impossible for words to express the heights of joy and depths of despair that have been experienced by the people whose stories are told in this book. Each person has struggled with his or her beliefs, programming, unconscious memories, religious and societal teaching, and soul love for many years.

We gratefully acknowledge the assistance of the clients, friends, and associates whose names have been changed; each story is true and accurate as presented. Your honesty and willingness to have your experiences told is courageous. We trust that your sharing will be healing to people who are struggling with guilt and/or pain in soul relationships.

CONTENTS

PREFACE

Why another book about soul mates? Because we see some important points missing from the writings and beliefs today.

Belief: I can visualize and affirm my perfect partner coming to me.

Not necessarily!

Much of the material written about soul mates gives this illusion. Visualizations and affirmations may assist in our opening to allow a relationship into our life. AND...these steps arise out of the Personality Consciousness. In this book, we want to stress that there is a difference between Personality Consciousness and Soul Consciousness. The people whose stories are depicted in this book were drawn together by a Universal Force beyond the participants' conscious awareness. Not one of them was "seeking a soul mate" at the time they met...they were guided by their SOUL.

Belief: When I meet my soul mate, I will have the fulfillment that I've always sought—it will be my "other half" and it will be passionate and loving 'till the end of our days.

Not necessarily!

The Soul does not always translate into physical reality the way our conscious mind interprets. Your soul mate is **mated to your Soul**, not necessarily your personality in this incarnation. You **may not** be together.

Belief: When I meet my soul mate, we will both be gloriously happy.

Not necessarily!

You may have killed him/her in a past life! There may be issues to be resolved. S/he may already be married... or thirty years younger, or older, than you, or of a different sex or culture than your preference.

Belief: Finding out about our past lives together will help me to understand what is happening between us; then it is resolved.

Not necessarily!

We are on a path of learning about love. If it is a soul relationship, the answer may not be (a) being together, or (b) walking away. The answer may be to keep your heart open to love.

A challenge? You bet it is! Especially when we are saying that being open to love means on every level of consciousness. It is relatively easy to understand and accept the concept on a mental level. Moving the love relationship with your soul mate through the emotional layer is infinitely more difficult. And, then, we are challenged to LIVE IT. To live, in this physical body and in this physical reality, the expression of our love.

INTRODUCTION

Soul mate: Romance! Eternal Love! Passion! Sexual Ecstasy! Is that what it is all about? Perhaps...and perhaps not.

The love between two souls may not always translate into the physical body according to our limited views.

An expanded view of love includes all of the above...AND also includes the love of two or more souls incarnating together to bring monumental life lessons.

Romantic or sexual love is only one expression of love. Your soul mate may be your mother, father, child, friend, lover, or spouse.

The reason we incarnate is to grow toward unconditional love. On that path, we move through all the experiences of "not-love," such as fear, greed, jealousy, possessiveness, control, hate, etc. As we experience what we need lifetime after lifetime, we bring more Light to our Being.

Simple? Apparently not! We can all say the right words about unconditional love...however, LIVING IT is not as easy as paying lip service to it. We are challenged every day to become more free...to become more whole...to become more Light...to become Love.

Your soul mate(s) may have returned to help you.

SOULMATE OR STALEMATE?

A new term has come into use that seems to have replaced those similarly confusing words such as boyfriend or girlfriend, lover, significant other, mate. Is the term "soul mate" simply a replacement word...or does it have a deeper meaning?

"I have met my soul mate!" a friend exclaims. She obviously is in the delirious and frenzied emotion of new love. A few months later when we meet her and ask about her soul mate, she might say, "Who?"

Many people are in love with love...the desire to feel and be with someone who makes their life exciting. When initial excitement wears thin, their need will draw them to more excitement. The search may continue endlessly, because no one can fill an empty space for another person indefinitely.

The term soul mate is generally described and imaged as lover in an ideal long-term relationship. If you are one of the fortunate people to have such a relationship, terrific.

3

A soul mate can ALSO be a
companion
friend
family member
close work associate
same sex or opposite sex
same or different skin color and culture

AND...A SOUL MATE CAN BE THE PERSON
WHO PUSHES US TO GREATEST SOUL GROWTH.

It is possible that a group of souls of like energy or
intent may incarnate together in order to forward a cause
or promote a movement; i.e., healing the environment or
awakening others through art. The energetic connection
may be referred to as a soul band...or soul fragments.
Some may meet in physical bodies; many will never meet.
If they do meet, it might be "comfortable" or
"uncomfortable"; however, major steps in growth are
likely to take place on their spiritual path.

It is also important to recognize that in all of these
relationships, growth is never one-sided. Movement is
always made on several levels.

Whatever the relationship may be in this life, the tie
is a deep inner connection that often seems to defy reason.

We have several soul mates...companions who have
been with us many times throughout lives, and know our
deeper self. We may meet one or two, or perhaps more.
One may be a close companion who helps us in our work
and/or life. Another may be part of a traumatic love
relationship that leaves us in the depths of despair. Both
may be soul mates.

PAST LIVES AND VIBRATION

Déjà vu, whose literal definition means, *already seen*, has been experienced by many and used in jest by most. Yet, in spite of its comical connotations and vague definitions, this word is still used to describe a sense of familiarity, of something that feels as if it occurred before. In a relationship the cause of a déjà vu experience may be the soul reacting to a previous incarnation.

As with any spiritual or metaphysical experience, there is no method of proving these phenomena, but their "real" feeling is undeniable. The very nature of a déjà vu experience suggests that a deeper knowledge and reality is penetrating the consciousness; in some cases this knowledge relates to a past-life experience or past-life relationship that may involve a degree of karma.*

---

*Cause and effect from past incarnations; in relationships, people being destined to learn or complete lessons from past lives.

5

We may refer to the initial recognition as chemistry. The chemistry is auric* energy reacting to another's energy, either adversely or synergistically. In the upcoming story about Matthew and Kevin, Matthew "recognized" Kevin at the first mention of his name. One person's aura responds to that of another, sometimes before meeting, and produces an internal response, a feeling of familiarity, appeal, attraction, repulsion, etc. This occurs in first introductions and in repeated daily interaction with very familiar people. This is the way we sense how another is feeling, and receive their messages of anger, sadness, amour, etc. AURAS DO NOT LIE!

Based upon an initial encounter, a relationship will or will not ensue. If there were past incarnations together, the previous experiences (including any non-resolutions) will be present in this "new" relationship. Although the chemistry may be compatible, the development of a spontaneous relationship is not always due to a previous incarnation, but may be due to auric harmony. In situations where past connections exist, we reanimate relationships for the purpose of resolution, or draw closely bonded souls into our lives to help us grow and stretch beyond our own confines. OFTEN, IT IS OUR STRONGEST SOUL MATES WHO HAVE THE ABILITY OR AFFECT TO PUSH US BEYOND OURSELVES FOR GREATER SOUL EVOLUTION.

These past experiences with others will invariably surface and become an active part of our life and relationships, again. They may be the primary reason for our re-joining in the first place. The initial causes and possible resolutions to karma instilled in a previous life are as limitless as the imagination. There are no right, wrong, more or less acceptable situations. All are legitimate and VERY real to the person who is

---

*Of a energy emanating from and around all living things.

experiencing his* karma.

It is an absolute misconception that because we have shared a previous life experience with someone or a group of people, we will **need** to be together again. We may simply need to meet and have a brief exchange. What determines a future together, or an ongoing relationship, is energy compatibility and possibly karma—things that are known only on a soul-consciousness level.

A commonly accepted universal axiom is, "Wisdom erases karma." The only problem with that basic, simple concept is that the acquisition of wisdom is not an easy accomplishment—particularly wisdom on all levels of consciousness. For most, the acquisition of knowledge in the mental layer of consciousness is a fairly easy process; however, incorporating knowledge into the emotional layer seems to be far more difficult. Even those who are comfortable with emotions can find this process anguishing. Unfortunately, the pain of growth cannot be avoided. It is not until knowledge is truly achieved on **all** levels that true wisdom occurs.

It is important to understand that there are no set rules or formulas as to how relationships should proceed. No one's internal experiences should be diminished, demeaned or judged. *Love is love is love!* Love is the REASON and NATURE of our existence. As long as participants involved in relationships have an intention of love, another's judgement is inappropriate. It is through pain that has been inflicted upon us **and** pain that we have inflicted upon others that we will learn greater love and grow beyond insensitivity and carelessness for life—in all its forms.

People come together because of their inner needs (spiritual and physical); the needs are compatible and suitable—they mesh. As inner needs change, so does the

---

*Pronouns he/she and his/her are used interchangeably throughout the text.

vibration. If that vibration becomes dissonant, we naturally seek another vibration. This change is not a threat to the other person except in the physical dimension, because such a change may take a person away. (There is always the possibility that needs may change again to where interaction with the original person is again harmonious.) Unfortunately, we do not easily allow relationships to move through those ebbs and flows out of fear of pain in the process or the end of the relationship itself. Relationships that are based largely on the physical level are less likely to stay connected. A spiritual bond holds potential that the person will again come into your life. As we focus on the constancy of the love bond, we focus less on how many days she is in our life or how many hours she spends with us; the bond becomes more important.

In terms of vibration or frequency, we can liken human compatibility to, as in musical tonal resonance, the attainment of either harmony or discord. We are made up of light energy, which vibrates within the Universal-light-energy spectrum. All energy operates out of an incalculable spectrum of tonal vibration. We "vibrate" and achieve either harmony or discord. This underlying element will set the pace or "tone" in relationships. However, relationships are never as simple as harmony or discord; we, as Beings, are far too dynamic for a concise positive/negative perspective. We occupy a band of frequency within that Universal spectrum, and we will seek those who vibrate within a workable proximity of our personal vibrational band. Though our energies are constantly in a state of flux, we are always "fine tuning" ourselves. And often it is dissonance that can provide that tuning, and prompt growth within ourselves. Also, it is often the dissonance that adds depth and even zest to our earthly existence. Sometimes, relationships will merely undergo a period of dissonance; later, harmony or compatibility may be re-established.

SOUL CONSCIOUSNESS VS. PERSONALITY CONSCIOUSNESS

Our energy consists of all of our thoughts, beliefs, experiences, and actions. WHO WE ARE is just that. We may put on a face or mask...but our true essence comes from our inner being. We change our energy and being—our consciousness—primarily through experience. And that experience, it seems, is what our soul goes through on the earth as well as in other dimensions and existences.

Our consciousness, then, evolves according to our connectedness to the God-Energy and our actions AND INTENT toward ourselves and others.

God-Energy is the Life-Force. We exist because of this force. Scientists have learned that energy does not expire; it simply transforms. As we leave our physical bodies (at death), our energy-essence moves into another form or dimension.

The separation between heaven and earth—spirit and flesh—heaven and hell—has been depicted by artists and writers since the beginning of time. Many religions have depicted the spirit as "good" and the body as "bad," and

11

for thousands of years humanity has tried to reach enlightenment or be more religious by connecting with God—and ignoring the physical body. Often religions become so caught up in teaching dogma that spirituality becomes secondary or is neglected altogether.

In the body, we do need to connect with the God-force...yet, we have never been disconnected from it—we simply are not aware or are out of touch with it. We cannot be disconnected—we are spirit, inhabiting a body. And, we do not have to DO anything to earn God's love; we are a part of that Divine Love—composed of that same God-love-energy.

In order to reach MORE love, more God, however, we have an opportunity to move from our darkness (we could call it blockages) such as anger, jealousy, possessiveness, fear, prejudice, etc., to more Light (wisdom and love). Our experiences, thoughts, beliefs, and programming—our unconscious memories—have created blockages. They prevent us from being more whole, more God-like, loving Beings. The only way to move through our blockages is to GO THROUGH them—and then, to live the new reality. Our soul mates help us (and in turn we help them) on the path to learning about love.

Due to strong programming, many people embrace the belief of failure in life. It is not possible to "fail" in life. We grow and evolve in life at a rate determined by our current abilities and willingness to push through our fears. When we are feeling failure with a situation, in truth we are probably experiencing **exactly** what we need to experience, so that we stretch and evolve beyond who we currently are.

The God-Force directs the soul to what it needs to experience. No one says, "This is the structure you follow," or "This is the program"..."Take this course before you take this course." Ultimately in the evolutionary and developmental process, with a direction for well-roundedness, we probably will experience all human qualities because they are basic to our nature. One person could learn jealously and it may be a one-time experience, and another person may need to live twenty lifetimes to work through jealously. The soul has a need to move and grow continually, while the personality often wants to remain comfortable in the physical experience. Some people in ho-hum marriages or relationships dream of passion and intensity. Yet those same people would run away from passion and intensity to stay with what is safe. For some, an experience in power is so profound that they get locked into that power. Another person may not get stuck in the power issue and could move to another lesson.

If we incarnate and internally conquer one single lesson, what we have learned is worth the experience. The exciting thing is that we take that knowledge with us. As long as we still have the ability to learn and change and grow, we will carry that new knowledge with our Being. Until our dying day we have the opportunity to make this life count.

The human experience is about growth and love. Unconditional love is not a vague concept; it is real. There is continuity and purpose to life. We draw souls to teach us something, and it is never one-sided. If we have resolved something and our partner has not, we will draw another energy to us. If she allows, another more appropriate person/energy will come to her as well.

We want to shatter the psychic's message that "It's going to happen," or "Everything is preplanned." Free will always exists. We also want to shatter the concept that we have complete power and control in our personality consciousness. It is only in the unification of the soul and personality consciousness that true power resides.

When our experience involves another person, we do NOT make choices for him. We cannot make the other person be where we want him to be.

At times we have heard a person refer to her soul mate saying, "I don't even like this person." If we are not relating to the personality, that can be so. The soul connection can be so different that we can feel we are dealing with two people. Even within ourselves, feelings can be so opposing that they do not make sense. Occasionally we recognize the soul...and do not identify with the current personality. When that happens, we need to understand that the personality is "more real" at that time—it has to be honored, otherwise we will keep running into a wall, thinking, "What happened? I don't understand." We may see into the deeper person, but we have to work with the personality. That is who she is at the present moment in time. It is this personality that she has to live; it is what the soul is working through. If two personalities are incompatible, a romantic or long-term relationship might not result. That does not mean that we do not have love for her, or that we do not have a soul connection. We may indeed have met a soul mate, but that does not always mean we will be together.

Sometimes there is a tremendous gap between the spiritual and physical dimensions. Until we become more integrated, that gap IS the reality.

We are creating on a spiritual level; we are co-creators with God. We are co-creating right now, and though we may not know **what** we are creating, we have basic inclinations that move us towards increased light and love. Companionship expands our ability to love and lifts our vibration to greater Light. We are moving to unity.

Swirling, encircling to enfold;
touching yet never touched;
longing, always fulfilled.

Reflecting, refracting within;
lines never drawn, boundaries never known;
clear, crystalline flows of light.

Fluid, flowing to engulf;
rising but never moving;
loved, loving yet always seeking.

When the soul needs to move and grow, and the personality in the relationship is not moving and growing, something has to break. Sometimes the personality gets a huge jolt and change takes place. Sometimes the relationship ends, to break the inner stalemate or to break an inner emotional dam. And, when we finally break through we do not go back.

The soul has wisdom and exists on a spiritual level in a lighter, freer realm or state of existence. But to experience that wisdom at a deeper level, we must live it in the physical. Often in order to learn a lesson we go to the opposite side; we learn through opposition.

We live in a multi-dimensional reality that includes layers and layers of consciousness. We simply do not have the ability to grasp the fullness of consciousness at this stage of evolution. To begin an understanding...or to give us a language...we speak about Spiritual, Mental, Emotional, and Physical layers. It is important to understand that there is not a place where a supposed spiritual layer ends and a mental layer begins, nor an imaginary line where the emotional layer ends and the physical layer begins. Every level of consciousness lies within every level of consciousness. Our spiritual consciousness resides in every layer, including our physical body; the body is spiritual. Our mental consciousness resides in every layer, including our physical body. So—there is not a separation of consciousness, but rather a holographic wholeness.

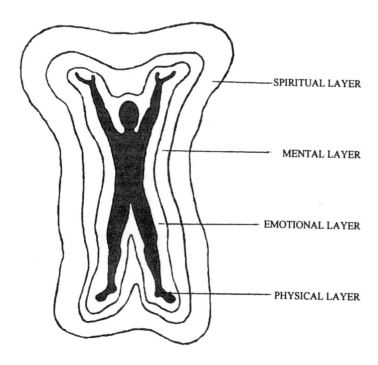

SPIRITUAL LAYER

MENTAL LAYER

EMOTIONAL LAYER

PHYSICAL LAYER

Our language is very limited when we speak about the soul. Nevertheless, our language is what we need to work with at this point in time. Language gives us a framework in which to discuss the movement of energy through consciousness.

As a spiritual entity, we are composed of energy-matter. If we relate this concept to materials, we can go from the densest material to the lightest that is still dense enough to remain part of that entity—it does not just fly off into nothingness. Those layers include the physical, the body being the most dense. The emotional layer is less dense, similar to water. The mental layer, lighter yet, like air...and the spiritual, the lightest, so light that we do not even perceive it in the physical. These layers are all inter-meshed, all part of the same, yet have separateness.

Because we have the ability, our consciousness can reside in aspects of these layers. We may move to intellect and become very mental in our perspective, shutting out emotion. We can become so mental we are cold and disconnected from our emotional nature. By being overly rational and logical about relationships and day-to-day activity, we move out of the joy and warmth of feeling in life. At other times we can reside in our emotion and not use mental faculties for balance.

The soul will find a way to evolve. If a person is out of touch with his spiritual quest and his journey is lived primarily through the physical, he will move at a slower pace but, of course, he will evolve.

It has been said that the spirit is housed within the body and the body is housed within the soul's consciousness. As we go deeper and deeper into the soul consciousness, we think of going "in." At the same time, we also use the term "higher and higher," as if going out externally. So, soul consciousness is "deeper into" and also "higher and away from." It becomes more expansive as we are more in touch with Universal reality— deeper inward and higher expanded.

When the energy does not move freely from one layer to the next, it usually means we get stuck. Some people enjoy the physical dimension—enjoying physical and sexual contact, joy, living comfortably in the physical world but are uncomfortable moving through the emotional layer. Some are comfortable in the emotional layer and not comfortable with the physical. People who reside in the mental appear aloof, not warm people, but analytical. And some who reside in the spiritual can appear as "space cadets," speaking in terms to which no one can relate. All are extremes and indicate potential imbalance. Because people can identify with a primary layer, if there is an imbalance, that is where they are likely to manifest problems.

When there is free-flowing energy moving through all the layers, blockages are less likely. We will be able to look at a situation from a mental layer, move it through the feelings, take action, if needed, in the physical layer, and stay connected to our spiritual awareness that there are reasons for what is happening in our lives. We can have trust that there is purpose in the spiritual dimension.

Moving energetically through these levels of consciousness is not as easy as it may seem. We can read something about emotion and relationships, and understand it, for example, the statement "Love means accepting another's path." Mentally we say, "Of course that's loving, that makes perfect sense." Then the lover comes home and says, "I'm leaving you, I met someone else." Emotionally we react strongly. Our emotions scream out, "Oh, No!" Mentally we have learned that it makes perfect sense to accept her path, but that acceptance does not necessarily translate in the emotional level. The lighter mental layer relates in understanding to the spiritual more easily than the emotional. The spiritual level has the greatest ability to understand. But on the denser physical level (in our example) we have not yet learned that concept to live it in this reality. We are moving slowly through energy levels. That is the reason to incarnate. When we have mastered a lesson in the physical, we have learned it in the densest level, and it is then fully a part of our consciousness.

IF OUR SPIRITS CANNOT MANIFEST LOVE AND PEACE IN THIS PHYSICAL REALITY...WE HAVE NOT LEARNED IT STRONGLY OR DEEPLY ENOUGH TO LIVE IT. We have reached true wisdom when we can incorporate love and peace into our lives.

Obviously soul consciousness is of the soul, exists exclusive of the physical, but also works through the physical. Though of different vibrational densities, all layers of consciousness are comprised of the same pure God energy. We speak about entering this life with blockages and lessons to learn—we'll call it "pre-programming" of the soul. Our task is to learn and develop certain aspects of the soul. So, the soul is housed in the physical. We come to the parents who can best help us learn particular lessons. We have the body, personality, astrological chart, genetics and culture—all these factors create the personality consciousness in this life and give the greatest boost for learning our lessons. The outer personality, like the body, is the vehicle the soul brings to work through the lessons.

KARMIC SOUL MATES
ENERGETIC CAUSE AND EFFECT

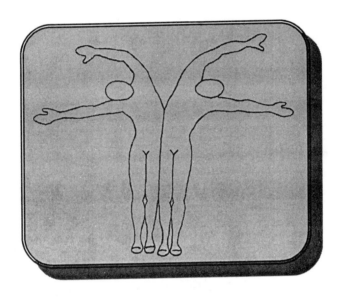

Created through Life Experiences

CAROL AND PETER
A STORY ABOUT KARMIC SOUL MATES

The karmic soul mate is one with whom we have "unfinished business," which could be a factor in many relationships but is primary between karmic soul mates. The two or more souls are drawn together because they did not resolve an issue in the past. This may be the most common relationship in operation today as we are taking steps to move beyond our lessons from past lives. The karmic soul mate is the one who can best bring the lesson...he or she is usually the one with whom we had the experience in the past.

When Carol and Peter met, she was 42 and divorced, he was 57 and married. Their time together would last only two and one-half years. It is best expressed in Carol's own words:

I learned so much about love. Peter and I didn't have a lot of time for our journey, but the amount of growth we did was phenomenal. The depth of love we had could never be comprehended by such a limited concept as "time together." I am still amazed at the number of people who equate the depth of love to the time spent together. How shallow and superficial that is. They do not understand the meaning of soul connection or soul history.

We look at marriages that have lasted thirty or fifty years—they stuck with it; it worked for them. But we cannot help but ask, "Did it really?" Yes, they are together. Yes, they are alive. And yes they care for each other, but there may be immense limitations. And we see the toll that such limitations took on those people. We cannot look at that and say that is where it is at...as much as we want to say, Yes, One And Only And Forever...because it is an aspect of human nature to want that.

It is so appealing to look at a couple who has been securely married for fifty years...they made a commitment, they stayed together, they had each other, and they were always there. And there is a part of us that says, "Wow, isn't that marvelous; I want that." But we think it is also honest and realistic to ask, "Was it best? Was it the most honest, loving, fulfilling, free space for love to grow?" And if we are going to be honest with ourselves as we look at many of these relationships, we will have to say no.

Neither Peter nor I really believed in reincarnation before we met. I had some questions about it and had been on a spiritual quest for a while, but had more questions than answers. Knowing Peter helped me to become a firm believer in past lives and karma. I spoke openly of my "new" beliefs and we had many discussions about it. He came to believe in it because our experience of this special and holy love that we shared was something that awakened that part of the heart that says "YES!" to the reincarnation belief. Our love is what awakened us to the belief, not vice versa. It really is true; an idea is an idea until there is an experience that gives it the power to make it a belief. Our love had a power that was incredible. It opened us both up to feelings and thoughts that we didn't even dare to imagine. The behaviors, both sexual and non-sexual, followed this change—this awakening of the heart and soul. It was undeniable, even though a lot remained unexplainable.

It was an instant attraction that can be fully appreciated only in retrospect. We came into the awareness of our purpose as we got to know and love each other—again. We were karmic companions destined for a union to confront unlearned lessons from past lives. Our conflicts were self-tests to see if each could let go of fear and respond with unconditional love. Also, could we accept each other without expectations, judgment or blame? The karmic structure of our relationship, I believe, was open-ended. The outcome depended on the growth of each of us individually. If we had both matured in love, then we could have remained together. But he stagnated and destroyed the potential for spiritual growth and set in motion the assurance of parting.

Peter loved his land and his farm. They were his roots, his connection to his God and his essence. He was both humble and proud of what he had built. He shared it all with others openly and freely. The first night we made love he took me to his favorite field and spread out a blanket under a clear star-filled sky. He wanted to share it with me so I could understand the inner stirrings of his heart. Our bodies were cool on the outside but burning with desire on the inside.

Peter was 57 only in chronology. He was a very vital man and in good physical shape; working the land and keeping busy helped him stay fit. His sexuality was something that surprised and astonished him. The power of spirituality-based relationships and love and love-making always blew him away—and me, too. He "performed" better than most 18 year olds. The emotional and spiritual satisfaction and joy were overwhelming and gave sex a dimension that neither of us had experienced or known before.

We had both been "dead" for a long time. I had been divorced for years and had turned to my work for diversion from loneliness and emptiness. He was married but the passion and affection had turned into a civil, business-like relationship many years before. His wife was content without the affection, attention and caring that the spiritual and physical aspects of love needed. Neither of us was consciously aware of looking for anyone or anything. We were both into the survival existence mode of thinking and feeling, or non-feeling. I think the great lesson here is that we do not have to understand or even know the journey, but just believe in the process and that God is directing it for our benefit. The mind or ego will struggle against that and question it to tell us we have to understand it before we accept it or open our hearts to it. That's a lie. People are brought in and out of our lives so that we can heal and learn the lessons of being loved and how to love, and develop our own spiritual selves in service to others.

Illusions of bliss haunt me,
gently making love from memories of life.
Wishful images of smiles, laughter and warmth
raise my soul to glorious heights.

Without warning a merciless predator descends,
attacking my unwitted frolicking joy,
floating effortlessly on currents of hope,
as a bubble created by the wishful breath of a child.

I fall, crushed under my own burden.
Left with seething wounds inflicted by the thorns of
dampened dreams.
Yet only a shell destroyed, hope reveals giving life.
A tepid glow remains, given in knowledge...
knowledge of another reality,

another time,

another place.

I learned the meaning of treasure and riches and it has nothing to do with things stored up upon earth. I think this was the main lesson that Peter came to learn. We shared a love that was beyond all comprehension or learning. The deep, spiritual connection that had been alive for many lifetimes together was once again alive, but not without problems. The conflict he had to resolve was one of making priorities. How much of a price was he willing to pay for his happiness, once he found what made him happy? He was a rich man materially and this brought him great comfort and security. He had built it himself, with the help of his wife and children. But he was very lonely, unhappy, sad and in despair, all under the guise of daily survival.

When we met I brought him a love that sparked his fire and passion for life once again. He did the same for me. Our worlds were turned upside down. He had a decision to make and the conflict he felt eventually led to his death—of congestive heart failure. He couldn't make the decision of the heart and soul. He wanted so much to make his home in love and joy, not civil, cool distancing. But to have the desires of his heart and soul he had to exchange part of his material wealth. He also couldn't negate *thirty-five years of companionship and obligation to his family. He could not permit himself to break the old connection with family and redefine one that had his happiness considered. He knew intellectually that his friends and children would understand, but fear ruled anyway. He could not see any way to have a win/win solution.*

I began by trying to force him to choose, but that only succeeded in driving a wedge between us. I finally learned to let go and just love him when I was with him. And how difficult that was! We both wanted to be together as much as possible—the joy was wondrous and beautiful and addicting, like a great thirst finally being quenched, marvelous and satisfying on so many levels.

When I stopped complaining that he wasn't there enough, he was able to get in touch with his own pain at not being there. He began to be the one who cried when he left at night. He was more in touch with the pain we both shared of leaving a warm, loving and passionate evening to go home to a cold bed and wife.

Having sexual intimacy without a committed living situation and without expectation is incredibly difficult in the emotional level. Partings come with every meeting—it is hard! **The commitment comes with and in the love, not the living situation.**

Peter's wife knew about his relationship with Carol. She chose to continue the relationship with her husband as married business companions. There had been no physical intimacy for many years. Carol, a marriage and family therapist, had her own personal struggle as she wondered if she was taking Peter away from his home. She came to the realization, *"I didn't take him away from home, I took him away from the bars."*

He began to come around more often because he was getting met his basic need to love and be loved. The choice was clear, but the decision was too difficult. His mind overruled the heart. The struggle was enormous for him. I could only stand by and watch. I could not make the decision for him. I could only love him with all my heart and hope that would be enough. It wasn't.

Peter went into a coma for five weeks, and it was the most difficult time of my life. I would drive 125 miles each day for maybe a few seconds of what I perceived as clarity.

*As if floating through a void...a tunnel
whose walls are lined with memories
of my past. I course through, gently
brushing against the supple rind while
the memories loom close, filling my being.
Bitter-sweet times...
painful tender moments, I continue...*

When Carol visited Peter in the hospital, his wife would often be there.

When I walked in, she would be sitting across the room looking out the window. I sat beside his bed and talked to him; I also talked to her, telling her how I remembered him. Even though he had told her about us, neither of us spoke about what my real relationship with Peter was.

He went home for a few days, and I didn't feel comfortable visiting him there. The lesson he learned then helped him five weeks later to make his decision. At home his wife had him in the living room, alone, while she left the house to go to work. After a few days, he went back into the hospital. I had the sense that he was doing some type of life review in the coma.

This time, Peter's wife gave instructions to the hospital that only immediate family was to be permitted in his room. Carol waited in the hospital chapel until his wife went home each evening, then she went into his room. The nurses understood what their relationship was, and saw the loving attention Carol gave Peter. They let her stay.

I had the inspiration one evening to take his favorite tapes and play them on his headphones. He and I shared a beautiful evening—our last. He thought he was back in my bedroom, sipping on a glass of wine with me and listening to the music. We spoke very briefly of our love and I asked him to take it with him. He promised he would. Since we both knew that we had been together before, I gave him my permission to do what he needed to do in this lifetime and that I would see him again soon. He understood. He said he loved me, slipped back into the coma, and died three days later.

I know that my love for him will never die. He will always have a special place in my heart. He took my love Home with him to use on his journey at a later time. We were brought together for a reason: to love and be loved. We both said what needed to be said at the time, whether it was acted upon or not. I could not have any expectations, for they are of the mind and interfere with the love of the heart. I could only love him completely, gently, honestly, and wholly when I was with him. And when he needed to stop his journey, it only reflected his own choices. It is what he needed to do. If he wants me to be on the next step on his journey, he knows I will agree. I cannot do his journey for him, but I can walk beside him and love him while he does it. And he can do the same for me. What an awesome privilege.

Approximately nine months after Peter's death, Carol wrote a letter to a friend who was struggling with a decision about her thirty-year marriage. They have both given permission to share the letter in this book. Following are excerpts:

Meaning doesn't lie in things. Peter could see that but was afraid to let them go. He didn't have the faith that is promised to us—that this Universe is abundant if we are open to it. Meaning lies in us, not in things. When we attach value to things that aren't love, we are loving things that can't love back. We are searching for meaning in the meaningless. Material things, of themselves, mean nothing. IT'S NOT THAT THEY ARE BAD. IT'S JUST THAT THEY ARE NOTHING.

We came here to co-create with God by extending his love. It is hard to live with someone in the role of mate (supposedly the closest bond) and yet not be able to share the essence of ourselves—our spirit. It tore Peter apart—yes, he let it by not trusting God and making a decision to go with his heart. His earthly teaching and fear kept him stuck.

How can I tell you that I hope for better for you? How can I tell you to release the old and trust the promise of the new? You will find love—how could you not? Can you really stop your journey to stay in what may be a spiritually harmful relationship just because you share a history?

I know you have difficult choices to make—one might consider them life-threatening. I will/do pray that you will have the wisdom and openness to do what your heart tells you. Peter denied love for history. He denied love for earthly obligations. He denied love for fear. He denied love for money and material security. He denied love of self and God. He denied his journey. He denied me...and he died.

Sometimes a successful relationship is the one that ends. When you have scraped the bottom of the barrel for learning and the bottom is empty—what purpose is there in continuing to scrape?

I pray you choose love and life, in whatever way it unfolds.

BLOCKED ENERGY DIMINISHES LOVE

Much of what is labeled love is superficial in that we do not expose who we are—our Inner Self. Many people are able to connect more with a platonic friend than with one who is a lover. Couples spend years of their lives together, every night sleeping in the same bed, and yet in many ways are total strangers because that Inner Self is not made known to the other person.

Many people stay in their intellect in relationships because it is a safe place to be—they control relationships so they cannot be hurt. When one senses that the situation requires an armor or strength, the mental layer is the place we go to guard ourselves.

Comfort with our Feeling Self is foreign to most people. A majority of people are fearful to be **feeling** beings. Basically due to past hurt, insensitivity and non-love, through eons of time, we have learned to build walls around us. Perhaps that was the reason behind the movement to a masculine energy-dominated society in the first place; that is a more guarded place to be. If one lashes out and hurts us, as a defense we shield ourselves. And so the more sensitive flowing side—the feminine side—has suffered, because the energy has been pulled back into the inner recesses.

God-Energy, the Life-Force is FREE-FLOWING ENERGY. Universal energy comes in through the crown of the body, down through the mind-body system including the legs and feet...then moves back up through the system to once again connect with the soul-essence of the individual.

We all have masculine (yang) and feminine (yin) energy. Yin is the receptive side of us that receives God-Energy and moves it through the system. Yang is the outward moving side of us that thrusts energy forward.

All energy is a part of the creative force of the Universe. Sexual energy is used to create babies, or a business, or a lovely home, or art...sexual energy is creative energy. Sexual energy is God-Energy. There is nothing else but God-Energy.

Our blockages limit the energy that flows through our system. Thoughts are energy, emotions are energy. Eventually those same blockages of energy, or thought-patterns, may create blockages in the physical body, blockages called illness or disease. The energetic blockages of love that Peter had lived for years contributed to deterioration, manifesting in the area of the heart.

We can only take in (receive...yin) as much God-Energy as our current consciousness will allow. That energy moves through the mind-body system freely—unless we block or limit it—according to where we are in consciousness.

Energy then begins the upward movement throughout the mind-body system. The "receptive nature" (to whatever degree one can open to receive) has taken in an amount of God-Energy. Now that energy returns through the mind-body system, moving back through the channels according to the "outward movement" (yang) nature of the person. Again, the blockages (fear, programming, inhibitions, beliefs, etc.) will affect one's ability to allow free-flowing energy, and/or diminish that energy flow.

COMPANION SOUL MATES
MUTUAL SUPPORT

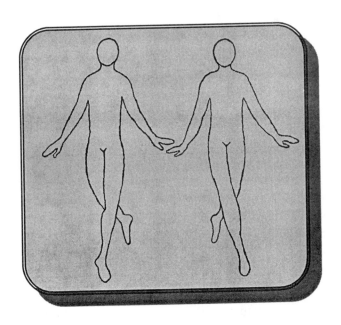

Created through Multiple Incarnations Together

ED AND JUNE
A STORY ABOUT
COMPANION SOUL MATES

Companion soul mates are those who have compatible relationships, and may have experienced former lifetimes, returning to assist each other. They have a deep understanding of each other's needs, and are able to be supportive through life changes and experiences, while, as in all relationships, providing opportunity for growth.

The soul mate relationship can be CREATED by simply living many lifetimes together, and for many people that IS the experience. By coming together again and again they find a compatible (on an energetic level) soul/person, and that bond continues to grow. They might return together in several more lifetimes because the bond has continued.

Ed and June have had a positive relationship from their initial meeting; she was a sophomore in high school, he was a senior, attending a different school. Even though it didn't happen until six years later, it seems that they both always knew they would marry. They raised their children in a happy and loving environment. Their relationship was one of support and trust—an astrologer would refer to it years later as "made in heaven." Ed gave June the safety and security she needed; June gave the same to Ed. What was lacking in one person seemed to be filled by the other.

We come to the time, however, when our souls seek that wholeness within ourselves, rather than through another. It seems that when one's soul pushes the personality to grow, it is not unusual for people to feel the change in energy between them. In the case of Ed and June, that change resulted in a separation that seemed to be required for their individual souls to create new patterns. While living together, they slipped into old habits that were no longer serving them; both would become frustrated. By living apart, each gained greater insight into their deeper selves, talents, abilities...and were challenged to "handle" the aspects of their lives that had always been filled by the other. For June that was in the area of independence and making her own decisions; for Ed, it was in the area of relationships and communication.

June started a new career. Although she did not yet earn enough to support herself, she was put into the position of making decisions without first asking Ed what she should do. Ed encouraged her and supplemented her limited salary.

In living alone, Ed needed to relate to people without the assistance of June; she had been the communicator. At times he preferred to be "a hermit," and at other times, he enjoyed social interaction. He began to balance his desire for a life of privacy and time alone with one of greater social exchange. June supported him emotionally and mentally as he shared his experiences with her.

June had a relationship with a man who lived in a different state; her focus remained on her career. Ed had several intimate relationships—exactly what his soul needed to experience. During this time, June and Ed talked often over the phone, visited each other, and made love. The love between them was never doubted, on either side.

If we set up a wall such as guilt over an affair, the guilt builds up an energetic wall. So even though there is love being exchanged, there is little being received in the way of loving energy. It is then filtered through the wall. Guilt tends to be the primary blockage in an affair.

By being honest, we are providing the spouse with an opportunity to grow. Honesty helps to break down the walls. Yet in these lofty concepts...not many could say in honesty, "It's okay, I understand." No—we are hurt. The human experience is not that light and loose. WE ARE NOT TO MOVE BEYOND THE HUMAN EXPERIENCE...WE ARE TO LIVE THROUGH THE HUMAN EXPERIENCE. We need to notice if we stop and get caught in a particular place. The human experience includes emotion—let's just not get caught there. By saying, "I would never trust him again," or, "It would absolutely change our relationship," we are getting stuck in the hurt: "I'm always going to be hurt by this and I'll never give you an opportunity to hurt me again," instead of saying, "I'm hurt and I want to work through this." It is an opportunity to grow in love.

When we realize that she can love another and it does not take away from the love between us, we have made major progress in understanding love—we are not threatened because she loves someone else. In June's words:

> Most friends and family members were totally confused. If they love each other, why aren't they together? Is there someone else? Did one of them have an affair?
>
> Yes, we did, but that has nothing to do with why we aren't living together right now. I told Ed about my relationship, and he told me about some

relationships that he had. I realize that we both needed something that we were not receiving in our marriage. What it means is that we could not give it—because if we could, we would have.

We must understand that what one could give to another when they met can still be given. What she could not give to him, she still cannot give. People think another relationship threatens. But does it really threaten? **We give what we can give and we cannot give what we cannot give.**

This touches upon one of the strongest misconceptions that we have—that one person should provide all that we need. When we make those vows, the person is to be our companion, best friend, only source of intimacy and only true source of comfort—that is nonsense. A person can give only what she can give; and we do have limitations. We may have greater needs than she can provide. It is tragic to deny love in our life, to not receive love from someone who can give it to us. If this love ends up threatening our current relationship enough that we have to let that relationship go, that is unfortunate. It is hard to be confident that love for someone else is not threatening the bond. If a person has a less-connected spiritual bond, other relationships do threaten what we share—if it is only a physical connection, it may break. Not every relationship is a deep soul connection.

Often relationships end because of hurt and rigidity, rather than because the person is no longer providing a need for us. We would rather discard the whole relationship than change or recalibrate it: "This is all he can give and I will not expect more." We still come out of "all or nothing at all." It is easier to let it go and revel in the hurt, or deny, in order to be monogamous. "It is okay to limit what my Being needs as long as I am faithful—faithful in this relationship no matter how much I am being denied."

If we hold to a rigid belief of all or nothing, we may create just that—nothing, never realizing the immense limitations we are imposing. Life is fluid. Even in a committed relationship, times of change and movement (such as having children, emphasizing a career) occur. There are times when we give less in the way of attention than at other times. Many mothers or fathers with young children face this difficulty when they simply do not have the same time or energy to devote to the spouse as when they were first married. Changeability in relationships is a very real cycle of life.

On the other hand, in divorce we hear, "I don't talk to my 'ex' anymore." It is a sore spot for people. It is that way as long as we are operating out of limitation. My "ex"—we do not acknowledge his name or existence —an X as if he were out of her life. "Do you have contact with your former husband/wife/lover?" "No, I don't think about him any more." She may either be blocked to that person's energy with a wall so she truly does not feel anything, or she may be in denial. If one pursues it, the emotion may come out in anger. We tend to not be honest when there is hurt involved. She may be setting up a karmic situation.

We are a collection of all our past experiences. Due to life circumstances we are restricted and have very real limitations. Although love in its pure form is free, we in the earth plane are not. We are hindered by personal and societal influences. Because of our restrictions we have limits on what we can give and what we can receive. And although we may *believe* we want and deserve more, our limitations will play a determining role until we free ourselves through the process of growth and evolution.

Comments from others have surprised me, June went on. *Several people (both men and women) told Ed "If she were my wife and wanted to live apart, I certainly would not help support her." Most of my*

*friends who knew could not believe that I was not
furious at Ed over his other relationships. I think that
they were venting their own anger; it wasn't mine.*

*How could anyone understand that it is an issue
of soul evolvement. It is not about sex, or money...it is
what our souls need to experience. Sometimes it
makes no sense to me! We love each other, and enjoy
each other's company. When our energy changes
began to take place, it was very difficult—Ed was
used to telling me what to do and I was used to taking
his word for everything, believing he knew what was
best for me. After living apart for several years, now
when we are together it is comfortable, as it used to
be. As strange as it seems, I know that it is right, and
that we are both growing through the experience.*

*Many married couples could never take this step;
it certainly goes beyond anything that we were
taught! After all these years, neither of us has wanted
to sign papers for a legal separation, so we haven't.
Our love for each other is very real. It is possible that
we will live together again; we have talked about it.
If we do, it will be important not to go back into the
old patterns—we had been married 25 years before
we parted, so those habits are deeply ingrained in
both of us. It is very difficult to change the way we
relate to a person.*

It is through separateness that oneness can occur.
The richer one's experiences are outside the relationship
the more wealth the person has to bring into the
relationship.

*I think we are attempting a new type of
marriage—one that is loving and supportive...yet still
can offer freedom for each other to do what is needed
for greatest happiness. This is no easy task...we were
both brought up with traditional values and it is hard
to go beyond that programming about what is "right"
and what is "wrong." I believe we are attempting to
move to a **higher love** than the confines of traditional*

marriage. I would be lying if I said it is easy—it has been extremely hard to do. Throughout the entire process, the only thing we were sure about is our love for each other. I think the astrologer was right, our marriage was "made in heaven."

Scents of an innocent past recall fantasies of hopeful inspired love. Moisture textured air gently presses against my distended, laden heart. Soft, muted, lighten tones reveal scenes of a time when disillusion was not yet known.

Today, I almost remembered to forget. A celebration of a love reborn an uncountable number of times. Born of the same fluid fabric, but sculpted into diverse garments. Not even truly recognized to the same, still love shared by the kindred grain.

Today, as forever, I love you...

LOVE IS...LOVE AS...

Since time began, poets, writers, composers, singers, artists, lovers and people in general have tried to understand what love is. We define love as an ENERGY, an EMOTION, a FEELING. Acknowledging love of country, love of nature, etc., the feeling of romantic love that moves between two or more human beings is the primary focus of this book.

In order to draw love into our lives we need to be willing to risk; however, if we risk with predeterminations and expectations, we are limiting the freedom of love's potential.

Two people are attracted to each other; the energies of their auras find like vibration. Assuming they begin a relationship, the energy continues to expand, diminish or change according to what happens between them.

So, these two people begin dating, and bask in the glorious feeling of "falling in love." They are connecting mentally and emotionally. At a point, a choice is made to make it physical. When this happens the energy moves into the lower centers of the physical body. (Note: We do not refer to "lower" as being "less than"; the term refers to a denser vibration in the physical body.)

At that point the energy between them makes a drastic change. An actual physical joining has taken place, and a stronger (heavier, denser) energy exchange has taken place between them. Depending on their choice of commitment, the relationship may include marriage or living together. The physical connection continues to grow, and it is not uncommon for the couple to begin to "meld" their activities, habits, thoughts, and beliefs. Sometimes couples who have been married for a long time actually begin to look alike. The energetic joining, as well as similar environment, foods, tastes, habits, and experiences all contribute to that phenomenon.

There is a creation of a third entity, so to speak, from individuals to "the Jones." Each will compromise to create a harmonious couple and family. Over time, the spontaneous or amorous energy between them dissipates as the energy becomes more comfortable —more identified as "same."

Love can be confusing in relationships as we misinterpret sex, possessiveness, jealousy, security, and/or power as love.

LOVE AS SEX

Making love and having sex are not necessarily the same. Sex for pure enjoyment between two consenting adults is just that—enjoyment and gratification. It may, or may not, include love/relationship.

As human beings, we are not free-flowing; our energy is substantially blocked. We can have sex and not give of ourselves. There are so many different degrees of energy that can be exchanged. In base sex there is an energy exchange, an obvious physical movement. For most lovers or spouses a greater exchange of energy takes place, but rarely does it go to the deepest inner space.

Moving to that inner space needs to include greater communication that goes beyond the sexual act, exchanging who we are through words, touch and sharing of our life at other times. And we bring that (or the lack of it) to the sexual act. If we are not sharing who we are—our likes, dislikes, hopes, fears, dreams—there is no way that we can be open in the sexual act because we have not even been open outside of sex.

Our society puts importance on physical intimacy as the greatest sharing. That is not necessarily true. We do not mean to undersell or to minimize it—physical intimacy CAN be the highest expression of love on the earth. But the hardest thing for people to give and/or receive is what we seek most—inner sharing. People who have numerous sex partners night after night have a hunger and a lack of fulfillment. What they are seeking is not going to be exchanged in the sex act itself. That act will become fulfilling when it is with someone who can share (and *when* he can share) the other levels as well. When we feel that kind of love and can move into our feelings and express them, life and relationship have more meaning.

And let's face it, it is easier to "Do" the sexual experience than it is to "Do" the inner-self sharing of who I am, my feelings, hopes, fears, dreams and desires. It is easier to have sex because we do not risk being open. There is no risk involved, (assuming we do not have blockages, where the sex act itself is a problem).

We have locked it all up in the one word called Love. But that word covers a myriad of things. It has lost its meaning; there is a belief that sex is love. The energy of love can be shared, but to make the statement that a deeper love was exchanged...not likely, especially in a society where we are not that open to exchange the energy of our inner beings in one night. Most people cannot be this open after knowing each other for an entire lifetime.

Exchanging the energy of our inner beings is making love. Exchanging energies in love-making is moving the energy of our being...moving it out of one and allowing it to flow into another and being receptive to the other person to allow the energy to move back into...that is LOVE MAKING LOVE—love expanding.

We have to recognize where our society and world is today. There have been places and times long ago, where energy has been more balanced and people were not as shut down. Today, one partner might allow openness during love-making for a space of time, but then withdraw when morning comes. All of a sudden the openness is gone, removed; they have withdrawn and put the wall back up. If a person becomes more integrated, he will not have to withdraw so much.

Frequently sex is used in place of communication. For example, a woman expresses that after conflict, if the couple has sex, the man thinks everything is okay. "We had sex so now everything is back to where it was before"...when communication has not taken place at all as far as the woman is concerned. Often, a multi-level sharing has not taken place. After this common experience, energetic walls rise between them.

If we want to communicate with someone, acceptance and receptivity on the other person's part is absolutely essential. If we sense judgment, a lack of acceptance, that sense is going to lessen how much we will share; we will close down. Every human being has experienced that. Unfortunately we feel it most often with the person we are closest to. Again it speaks of the limitation that we experience in that most important, most unified relationship. So, the sexual expression of love "naturally" occurs less and less often. Aside from the obvious decreased passion from initial beginnings, etc., this reduced sexual activity is often accepted as the aging process. We do not agree.

In our society it is accepted and expected, (which is horrendous programming) that sexual interest and ability diminishes with age and familiarity. Yet, in truth it may not be age at all, but the vitality of the relationship which is diminishing. Other than a lack of physical health, if the sexual relationship in marriage diminishes as the couple becomes older, this change is due to diminished energy exchange between them. Impotency is often a result of blocked emotion and the presence of energetic walls between the couple. Once built, a wall is not easy to break down.

LOVE AS POSSESSION

Why does "my" husband, wife, lover, mate change from a word of identification to ownership? A large amount of energy is focused in the second chakra* (sexual) and first chakra (security). Physical choices to be together usually involve joint ownership of material possessions...and...marriage (even living arrangements) become LEGAL CONTRACTS.

In our current practice of love as possession, if one's mate falls in love with another person, the common response is to feel threatened and/or rejected, angry, fearful, resentful and desiring to punish. Those actions are the result of a belief in owning and possessing love.

_____

*Spiritual energy vortexes connecting with the physical body.

LOVE AS JEALOUSY

Jealousy has been misinterpreted as "He cares!" We desire emotional responses from our partner. Erroneously, we make him jealous, to reveal an emotional connection that we seek.

In reality, jealousy shows insecurity. In the earthplane it appears that jealousy may be an innate vibration at this time. In other cultures and periods there have been varying degrees of the jealousy vibration. When and if it occurs to you, recognize your internal reaction; the important factor is how we respond.

Anytime we worry about something, we are holding onto it. If we are worrying about losing someone whom we love, we are not allowing freedom of the energy for her to fulfill her potential. When the fear of losing someone is so great, we can make that loss happen; it can become a self-fulfilling prophesy. There are relationships filled with jealousy unnecessarily...after years of fear, suspicion and accusation, it is not unusual for the mate to eventually have an affair.

LOVE AS SECURITY

We find security in the person who has qualities or skills that are lacking in us. For example, the woman who believes her earning power to be minimal might seek a man who appears capable of supporting her financially. A man who lacks communication skills might seek a woman who will fill that gap in his personality.

The unconscious attraction to another to fill our needs is initially quite gratifying. In a positive relationship, we can benefit from the energetic exchange of the other...and, we hope, become more whole. If we do not incorporate these qualities for greater wholeness, but instead continue to lean upon the mate, love will become dependent, "I can't do without him." Even our love songs ENCOURAGE such dependency!

LOVE AS POWER

Money, a good job, a promising career have been interpreted as love. We wonder how many young women or men distorted a lack of power into love for one who appeared to possess power.

If we and another soul have had several lifetimes together with an issue of power, there seems to be a connection on that consciousness level. We return on that level until it is transmuted, severed, or changed. Until then, the issue remains and it will guide our relationship. It will be a strong issue; it could manifest as an overbearing parent, spouse, business associate— whatever is set up. But there is always going to be a power struggle until we are able to resolve and transcend it. The issue will keep leading us because there is a lack of resolution from the past.

So souls come back together in order to go through lessons to learn about the issue of power...until we are able to balance and have equal power. If we reach wisdom in that issue and our partner has not, we can then draw into our life someone who has different energy. We will no longer need to focus on the power issue. The other person can continue to work on the issue with someone else.

Ultimately that is how these people serve in our lives. We can resent the person for being so controlling, or recognize that this is an opportunity to move into our own power. She cannot have control unless we let her.

THE ISSUE OF TRUST

"HOW CAN I EVER TRUST HIM AGAIN?" is a common question after one learns about an affair. It is coming from a perspective that an intimate relationship requires a physical commitment FOREVER. Would she react the same way if her mate had a mental love or an emotional love for another? We seem to narrow it down to "Is he having sex with someone else?"

It seems physical intimacy is what we care about, even though a mental, emotional or spiritual bond can be much more powerful than "having sex with someone." But that is where we put restrictions; we can accept that our mate may have a bond with another, but cannot accept their sharing physical intimacy. If that occurs we feel that our trust has been violated.

The issue of "how can I ever trust her again," comes from the promise of "I will love no one but you." The truth is that we can never make that promise unless we intend to limit our soul growth. No matter how enlightened, how great, how advanced a person is, one human being can only offer what he can offer—his perspective, his energy, to another person. If we limit ourselves to interaction only with him, we are limiting ourselves to that experience. And we do that by standing at the altar saying, "I agree to limit love."

People devote immense amounts of energy to that limitation. Drawing a person into our life reflects an inner need that our current relationship is not providing. Likely, a month from now our relationship still will not be capable of filling that need.

And yet, if the two people standing at the altar can acknowledge that love expands as we open our hearts, they could allow life (and trust the Universe/God) to bring what it does. Then their love can expand. They can grow as much as they possibly can because they give each other freedom to allow what comes into their lives. Some people have the potential to do that, but because the programming is so rigid, "You are mine, I am yours, I possess you, you possess me," that we cannot even think along those lines.

We become One is a concept of losing ourself in the interest of becoming a better or larger entity by merging with the other person. If we limit that concept to the physical dimension and our mate goes toward another person, we feel that our mate's action destroys what we have built.

WE NEED TO REACH THE POINT WHERE WE CAN SAY, "I TRUST YOU TO DO WHAT IS RIGHT FOR YOUR SOUL."

That is where the trust level has to be, otherwise we are imposing **our needs** in the trust. We are saying, "I trust you to do what **I want** you to do." In that way we are saying, "My trust in you is dependent upon what I think you should do out of my own need." It is more expansive and moves toward unconditional love to be able to say, "I trust you to do what is right for you. I trust you to do what you need for your soul growth." We can still be in the love of each other, but with greater freedom in our life journeys.

It is in the atmosphere of freedom that love can truly exist and grow, and THAT is when we can trust that the love will always be there...not trust that the person will not find another, because that may not be true. But we can always trust that the love will last...and that is the kind of trust that we seek and toward which we need to move.

LOVE IS...

Though it may be deeply heartfelt, the verbal expression of love may represent limitations, such as need, insecurity, fear of being alone, etc. A great deal of fear can be masked behind "I love you."

Some people think love means always being there for another. "Being there" does not mean responding to every whim. But when the need is real, it is not unreasonable to ask. We can do that for each other if there is a real honesty and sensitivity in the relationship. We must, however, be willing to respect the position of our mate in what he can provide. If it truly is not best for him, then it is not fair to expect him to be there.

When we authentically love ourselves, then—and only then—are we truly free to give love to another. **We cannot give what we do not possess.** As long as we think/act out love as possessiveness, jealously, security, sex, or power...we will not reach into ourselves to experience Self Love.

It is said that we see the God-Force in the lover and that is why we connect with another person. Our opening to love opens us to God. If we can open our heart more, we open to God-Energy. We have a need to know ourselves and give love to ourselves; however, initially it seems the only way we can do that is to give love to someone else so she can give love back to us.

It may be that the First Stage of love is finding someone to love because we cannot love ourselves. The love we send out comes back to us. The Second Stage is learning to love ourselves. Stage Three is learning to love the greater whole—humanity.

TWIN SOULS
ORIGINAL CREATION

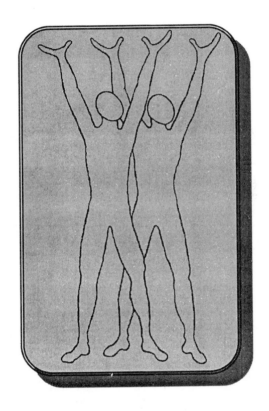

Created in the Spiritual Dimension

MATTHEW AND KEVIN
A STORY ABOUT TWIN SOULS

The term "twin flame" or "twin souls" has been used to refer to that soul-counterpart, the "other half" of us. It has been referred to as a birthing or soul splitting. An original soul division might split into two or more parts. This category is popularly referred to as Soul Mate. This person is the one for whom we search, the one who makes us feel complete.

This soul mate relationship could be present with the person who appears most opposite to us (the "other half") and feel like a completion of all that is missing in our Being. On the other hand, the person could be strikingly and disturbingly similar. Either way, one sees a reflection of himself and a longing to be with the person, to reunite, not just to be together or to share, but almost to "go Home." We have heard the statement "Home is where the heart is," and this is true. We must come to the place of understanding that home is not four walls or a building. Home is where the heart connects to the soul.

Although life on the earth is a temporary experience, true love from the heart/soul is not temporary. We are always being challenged on earth to respect the ever-changing nature of life. When we become attuned to the greater truth, we do not feel so threatened. In Matthew's words:

> *I felt that I knew Kevin before I even met him. When a friend wanted me to meet his date, he spoke Kevin's name and it prompted feelings of knowing ...and at that moment I knew that I had to be with him. Several days later my friend introduced us; Kevin and I talked and talked, as my friend melted into the background.*

We have communication and connection with many people throughout our lives. What makes one soul special to us? Our feelings tell us that with certain people there is an absolute difference. We respond internally to the mention of someone's name, to the thought of that person, and we experience a consistency in the internal response.

With other people, feelings can be strong or intense, but we are responding in the here and now; we react because it is what we are feeling. The connection is clear and our reactions make sense.

With eloquent expression we silently move;
life's warm essence ever flowing through.
Soft shapes glimmer in a green of hue;
diffused light shimmers in a vastness of blue.

Through crystalline eyes we touch the soul;
ever longing to meld as on...we know.
With loves caresses our hearts sing life's song;
in gentle harmony forever we long.

As if a child we frolic in life's love;
moving, dancing, resting as one.
Created as light that flickers through life we breathe;
with soft comfort we merge, one...we are to be.

Matthew is a man in his early thirties; he has dark hair, dark eyes, and dark complexion. Kevin is in his late twenties, an attractive man with fair complexion, blond hair, and blue eyes. Their physical appearance is strikingly opposite when they are together.

From the very beginning, the relationship with Kevin produced feelings of familiarity and comfort for Matthew that no previous relationship ever had. Yet, as the relationship developed and time went on, other less desirable, unexplainable feelings started rising. Matthew sensed that Kevin did not trust him, a feeling inappropriate to the reality of the situation. Not long after they had begun an intimate relationship, Matthew began to have feelings of "owing."

> *I felt as if I wanted to be forgiven...and that was bizarre—why on earth would I want this person to forgive me when there was nothing to be forgiven?!*

Even though Matthew felt that he was unwaveringly committed, attentive, and loving, he was the one with the burning sense of owing.

One of the major differences between a soul connection and simply a past life together is that with a soul connection we have feelings that may not be logical or rational. The feelings might not correspond to the current situation.

As the relationship continued, Matthew's emotions became stronger and stronger and eventually Kevin started pulling away. Kevin focused on his own career; Matthew focused on the relationship.

At the time, the disappointment and increasing feelings of rejection became intolerable. My logical mind said, "Get out!" but my heart screamed with opposition to that suggestion. I did finally make the decision to leave the relationship. Before this decision became irrevocable, my attempts were many and spanned a period of several months. To make the decision final, I even decided to leave the area where I was living—a place in which I felt a real sense of belonging. This separation had a more profound effect on me than I ever could have imagined.

I realize now that the logical insistence to exit the relationship had combined with a deeper soul prompting in order that I might collapse the enormous emotional dam I harbored. I firmly believe that no other Being could have effected these results. My greatest need in my well-being was to have my emotions freed.

Prompted by intense emotional distress, Matthew sought a past-life regression. He found that part of his karma had been instilled during a life in Renaissance times. Matthew had been the son of a wealthy and powerful man in business and politics. The person he loved (Kevin in this life) was a peasant, and thus their relationship was forbidden. Matthew accepted his father's (and society's) position and broke off the relationship, never seeing his love again. He inherited his father's wealth and filled his life with love of money. He died an extremely lonely, wretched man.

In this life, money and power are important to Kevin; they are not important to Matthew. The strongest pull of his life was the desire to be with Kevin.

I have never met anyone who has moved me as deeply as Kevin. I don't think I'll experience anything to that depth again.

If I had a wish this day
as in past through fluent eyes you'd see,
days and nights, ebbs and flows from heart
without pale, life committed free.

You'd remember a past
before regret and scorching pain-filled vow,
succulent, glimmering shapes entwined
love shared, only united souls could allow.

Yet the veil that now cloaks you,
wears thick to calloused, sutured end,
neither vigil nor passion's flame can pierce
in spite of ceaseless pleas to amend.

Through final bewailed blaze
upon winds I cast bounds to heaven's dome,
from a fathomless soul's heart I pray
once freed, love's currents will wish you again home.

After they parted, Matthew sank into a severe depression. His friends worried about him. He felt unable to function for a period of time. Past-life therapy helped him to understand *"that I'm not crazy,"* and that his intense emotions were a response to another lifetime in which he had put money over love. He wanted to be forgiven and to "repay" Kevin; however, Kevin had his own agenda—at least a part of which is to have money and position in this life.

Matthew continued to search for the overwhelming connection that he felt to Kevin.

> *If I allow myself to move into the reserved, feeling place in me which is Kevin, I can sense/touch him there and know how he is doing. I know our love can live there in freedom—in that place where there's no space or time.*

It simply went beyond anything that he was accustomed to or had the capacity to do with anyone else.

In another regression, he moved to a place where he and Kevin had been twins.

> *The scene opened in a very lush tropical setting. I sensed it to be Polynesia. There were grass or reed-type huts in a village that was not far from a waterfall and small lagoon that I sensed to be my secret, favorite place. I saw myself as a young male, about 10 or 12. Although I regularly went to my secret place alone, I was most frequently with my twin brother, Kevin in this life; we were inseparable. We often played with the other children in the tribe, but the "secret pool" was where we would always end up.*
>
> *The waterfall was fairly narrow, but had substantial height to it. We repeatedly climbed the step-like rocks of the waterfall's edge and would then jump or dive into the deep blue-green water of the lagoon below. As I moved a bit further into the regression, I saw my brother climbing higher up the walls than we had ever gone. I became alarmed and frightened and started yelling up to him, but he ignored or didn't hear me. He then slipped on a*

moss-slimmed rock and fell. He couldn't catch his balance and was pitched into the rocks below and was killed. All I remember then was seeing myself floating face down in the water, dead. In grief, I believe that I drowned myself.

Matthew has had several psychics (in unrelated places and times, and without any foreknowledge) see him and Kevin as an original cell or as a twin being. It would seem that this type of soul similarity often, if not always, manifests in the physical as an innate sense of knowing and closeness on a feeling level.

Feathery soft bracken whose sweet lofty breath,
speak in quiet hushed tone;
while suspended from below a blanket of moss,
suppress their subtle drone.

My gentlest friends with ever attentive heart,
hear the songs never sung;
taking then giving from depths rarely known,
spoken in tones silently rung.

Yet I know other times another place,
where tree and sky make bond;
elegant green but on top,
a shock of clustered frond.

Borders of sand alabaster white,
encroaching on the blue;
warmed by a star precariously close,
a friend, loving, true.

Then the place my heart of hearts,
how I wish to forget;
for now is not the time to remember
with absinthe/blue regret.

Kevin began a new relationship and moved in with that person, something he had not been able to do with Matthew. Matthew began a new relationship—with himself. For the next two and one-half years, he went on an inward journey to discover more about himself and the mental, emotional, and spiritual ties to the soul whom he recognized as Kevin.

At times it became so clear; I knew that our souls were joined. Other times I raved at my pathetic need to make more out of that relationship than what it was—it seemed so obvious that he felt no such tie to me. As time passed, even with no contact, my feelings remained. I learned about the extreme difference between our soul connection and what was happening in "real life." I had to accept that Kevin's soul has its own path to follow, and that it (at least now) only minimally includes me. He has a need to be successful and to have money; perhaps my soul needs to feel how he felt when I left him in the Renaissance lifetime.

I have decided that I will do my best not to close my heart and love to him, although I'm certain that

*my soul has already decided this. I wish to know
greater freedom within and I know that completing
any karmic lessons in this life is part of that process.
Also, I very much want to learn about unconditional
love.*

Matthew's two and one-half years were spent
releasing mental and emotional blockages that had
surfaced from his relationship with Kevin. He underwent
past-life regressions, body-work,* and spiritual
counseling. He wanted to reach the point of greater
unconditional love—and in this case, that meant **letting
go.**

Eventually, as Matthew felt ready to allow more love
into his life, he met William. Only through another
relationship could he understand that giving love to
William takes nothing from his love for Kevin. There are
factors in his relationship with William that were not
possible with Kevin.

We asked Matthew if he thinks William is a soul
mate.

*No, or at least not in the same way as Kevin. I
remember when I met William, I felt no attachment to
him...or if I did, it wasn't a situation like "There's
something I need to resolve here," as with Kevin.
William and I are compatible, we provide love and
companionship, but one of the key things we do is
mirror each other. I can often see myself and how I
reacted to Kevin in how William reacts to me now.
And it helps me to better understand Kevin's position.
With William, it is a loving, complementary
relationship that provides the opportunity to learn
greater balance.*

---

*Polarity, energy balancing, deep muscle massage, etc.

Matthew has gone through many internal stages dealing with his love for Kevin. Occasional cards or telephone calls only made the pain of separation worse. He needed some space and asked that Kevin not contact him. After more internal healing took place through mental and spiritual understanding, he felt stronger and more balanced emotionally. Now they have occasional contact as friends.

...in my heart of hearts, I adamantly believe that I will never be fully happy until I can freely share the love that I once so foolishly lost and now ache for like nothing else. I'm told that love is never lost if you truly believe in it. Love for self and patience will allow it to freely come back. If this is true, and I must believe that it is lest my life be a sham—I wait.

His crystal fluid realm lies gilded
in frosted muted hues,
the warm refracting gem lies low
beneath translucent eyes of ice and blue.

Sealed safely secure
banished far to depths unknown,
this loving heart once risked in being
before scattered and foolishly thrown.

Now a time without bounds I languish
to love this imprisoned heart free,
reminiscent of a life that once swelled and flowed
an immutable vow to again resonate in "B."

What about the future for Matthew and Kevin? We believe that the future is not SET. Our daily thoughts, intentions, feelings and actions affect our future. Although psychics, astrologers, etc. can provide valuable insights, they cannot pronounce a rigid, predetermined future. Psychic seeing, ideally, offers clarity in possibilities and probabilities; however, it is through LIVING that we create. We want to promote responsibility, sensitivity and living in loving respect. **We create our future in our day-by-day choices.**

FREEING EMOTIONS

As human beings we are often blocked and fearful, not able to share our deeper selves out of fear and conditioning. Because of that, it is difficult to feel the greater expansion of love that lasts...and yet that is what we seek. We continue to search for it in another person. What we need to do is find it in ourselves AND be willing to be vulnerable to share with another. Whenever we block emotional energy, not only have we lost touch with our own loving feelings, but we also lose the ability to receive love from another person.

There is a lot of neediness; the need for emotional connection and interaction is so strong, many people "force" the experience through the bar scene, dating services or Internet, and find themselves let down and disappointed.

Some people are not open to emotional energy and try to find fulfillment through work. Work brings a fulfillment to certain aspects of ourselves but is not a substitute for intimacy. To try to find emotional **love** fulfillment through a job is not possible. Often what people do is work harder—they work for success even more in an attempt to fulfill what they are seeking, all the while feeling less fulfilled. When we over invest in one aspect, we may be denying something else. And that denial may manifest in our lives as imbalance resulting in financial success with an emotional void.

One cannot escape oneself. Avoidance through working, traveling, moving, or the excitement of a new relationship gives a false or temporary sense of accomplishment and relief from inner pain.

An example of avoidance is the man who represses his own emotion and experiences it through the women in his life. Often this personality has drawn someone into his life to carry his emotions. The resulting relationship is not always best—he needs to be in touch with and take responsibility for his own emotional being. In this example, the woman may take on the role of caretaker. Caretakers try constantly to "protect" loved ones from experiencing emotions. Making it "okay" is not necessarily a loving act.

On the other hand, some people live so deeply in their emotions displaying a lack of control, that everything else becomes secondary. Emotional excess can cause a person to become dysfunctional due too their over reactions and inability to be present. This extreme imbalance is generally difficult to be around if not altogether intolerable..

We need to be balanced enough to determine how open the "receiver" is to our love/ energy/emotion and to recognize if our emotional output is appropriate to the receiver's ability to accept. When a person has an overload of repressed emotionality, she seeks a recipient with whom to attach. A person in this position cannot understand that no one person can be the receptacle for her emotional surplus—she becomes smothering. When she has released enough emotion to be more integrated, she will find someone with whom she can share a healthy relationship.

One's fear of a relationship ending can actually push another away. This fear is as much of an extreme as that of a person who has totally removed his feelings and become immersed in work—an analytical, automaton walking through life. The balance we are seeking can be found in using the mind to recognize more objectivity in our perspective while using communication and other forms of release, such as artistic or creative endeavors, to free emotion. Talking, moving energy out in all forms, is healing.

Communication is the life blood to a healthy relationship, yet it is also imperative to respect a person's decision to not communicate.

A common problem which often arises where non-communication is present is when the significant other is the source of the difficulty and therefore "too close to home" for discussion. The interaction is intimidating; the person to whom we need to talk may be non-receptive. It is not unusual in the case of a couple that one partner may not have anyone close to him because his marriage has prevented friendships with the concept "My spouse should be my best friend and everything in the world." So he stores his emotions and adds resentment. Such an interaction creates people who coexist and are blocked toward each other.

When Matthew was struggling in the relationship, Kevin would not communicate on the level desired. Matthew needed honesty, and although it was very difficult finally to hear, "You're not the one for me," that was what Matthew needed. Honesty is always deserved.

In relationships, it is not always possible to dissipate blocked energy through communication. It has been proven that another means and/or aid in releasing blocked energy is the use of one's creativity. Emotional storage can be expressed and substantially reduced through creative ventures.

Our deepest emotional responses are triggered by soul mates—no one else pushes us in the same way. Whatever the issue, the key is to work on ourselves, and to integrate **all** layers of our being.

STAYING OPEN TO LOVE

By nature we have a need to relate—to give love and receive love; that is a part of the human experience—a need to exchange energy. Love is energy. When we deny that part of us, it is like denying ourselves food—hunger increases. The need/hunger left unattended continues to increase, until one day it cannot be contained any longer. The desire to satisfy that hunger then becomes the greatest focus in one's life. This unmet need could arise later in that life, or it may not surface until another lifetime. It may also manifest in the body as illness or dis-ease.

A deficit can result from not receiving love as a child. If that pattern is set up, one learns to keep denying love. He will not allow love, because he has a subconscious belief that he does not deserve it. He may bring love to himself, then push it away. He might seek fulfillment only through sex, but when emotion rises, have difficulty dealing with his feelings.

A deficit in love companionship or relationships can cause neediness. The severity of this neediness will determine how one relates. Neediness can be so strong that a person will not be able to have a platonic relationship. Relationships will always move toward the extreme, "This must be the one."

Many people marry in that initial synergistic experience. They are caught up in, "He is the one and only—I found Mr. Right," and a few years later realize, "I can't do it any more, this just isn't good," or "I'm married so I have to make it work."

How do we stay open to love? How do we keep love open yet not hang on to the person or wish for something that is not reality? It is not done through a mental decision. Through the process of remaining open and in touch with our feelings, allowing the feelings to be vented through writing or journaling, counseling, talking our friends' ears off, etc.—in that process we are freeing ourselves of excess emotionality. Demands and expectations reside in that excess emotionality. As we release it, our perspective begins to shift and we can see the person more clearly. The love may be very real, but we need to release expectations that hang on in the emotional layer.

How do we avoid closing the door on love? When a person is telling us something that we do not want to hear...try saying mentally, "I want to listen to what she is saying because I respect her perspectives and feelings. If I can't listen, she will become inhibited and close down and a rift may form in our relationship." Be open so that she can share in the way that she could with a close friend. Try to verbalize, "I want to be able to be there for you, but I am experiencing this inside. Let's work with this, don't close up on me, I'll try not to close up on you." Remember, it is unrealistic for us to think that we can be everything to another person. We have limitations. We cannot be **all** things to anyone.

Matthew is continuing to create love in his life. He is not creating fear, resentment, or hate; he is creating love. Unfortunately, the most common reaction when a relationship ends is to feel anger and vengeance. The hurt and anger are normal to experience at the change of a relationship. These feelings need to be acknowledged and dealt with, but they do not need to be fostered.

What is an acceptable way to move anger? Well, raving like a lunatic moves it very quickly. But that kind of behavior is hard for people to take, even if the anger is not focused on them. We can use our intellect to avoid raging AT A PERSON, but we can rage ABOUT A SITUATION. If we say, "Okay, now this isn't worth getting angry over," or "Rise above it," we **may** be suppressing our anger. Even though we may feel as if the anger has passed, it will not dissipate without attention. This anger could emerge as depression at another time.

When we recognize fear, it must be confronted to grow beyond it. Nothing conflicts and inhibits love more than fear. We must confront fear in order to stay open to love. More than any other emotion, fear shuts down the heart and paralyzes the soul.

SOUL UNION
SOUL MATTER EXCHANGE

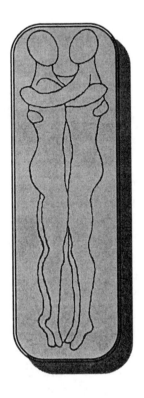

Created in the Physical Dimension

MORGAN AND SUZANNE
A STORY ABOUT SOUL UNION

Love energy by nature is unconditional. It is unbiased and does not impose limitation or rule. If allowed, it will be directed by its nature and find a synergistic complement. Only humans in our fears limit love and its potential. Race, religion, gender, marital status—all structure, does not exist in love.

Morgan and Suzanne met after both of them were married. Between them there was an energy intensity that was a combination of attraction/repelling. They argued over everything from religion to politics to the weather. Suzanne, a rather passive woman, felt shocked at her spontaneous reactions to Morgan and how she spoke up and argued with him—something she had never done with anyone else.

Morgan's attraction to Suzanne kept pushing him. At his admission of love to her, Suzanne exclaimed, *"You can't love me; I'm married!"* *"Suzanne, I'm married too,"* he reminded her.

Yet as he continued to pursue her, Morgan felt confused, too. Once he said, *"Suzanne, I love you, but I*

76

don't know if I like you." Suzanne told him the attraction was only an infatuation. *"This was impossible —absolutely impossible. I would NEVER have an affair, and an affair with a married man? Not me! Never!"*

In spite of Suzanne's conviction, an affair is exactly what insued...and she still could not believe it was happening. What was this incredible intensity between them?! Even though he had pursued her, Morgan equally struggled with strict Catholic upbringing and guilt about his marriage; he had never had an extra-marital relationship before.

I remember him sitting on a couch and in great turmoil, his head dropped into his hands as he whispered, "Why didn't I meet you first?!"

Over several years, Morgan and Suzanne had an on-and-off-again relationship. Guilt would break it off and then they would be drawn together again. Morgan said *"I'm willing to be Number Two."*

I long to touch you with my heart, my soul.
I long to lie beside you, warm you with my love,
touch you with the stars. Your bright glistening eyes
beckon me close, but I can only touch you in the dreams I
wish to share.

I've seen water, glossy, warm trickle down your subtle curves. Water refreshing memories of another time, another place. Remember gently, listen intently, you'll hear the songs of our heart; bending, curving, arching in love... gliding silkily in life's gift.

You run from me, hiding, peeking, like the ever gentle rain that fell from our sky. Turning blue to green and back again. I know you remember light reflecting, refracting, crystalline eyes piercing to soul...knowing, understanding, being.

Suzanne told us:

> *I had to understand this. It made no sense. I loved my husband, he loved his wife. We were both in marriages we had no intentions of leaving—such a discussion never took place. The truth was, my relationship with my husband was more comfortable than the intense energy between Morgan and me. Yet, in spite of every obstacle, the relationship continued.*

At one point communication ceased for a twelve-year period while Suzanne and Morgan were involved in their separate families and Morgan focused on his career. During that period they spoke on the phone perhaps once a year as a social exchange...but the relationship was, in Suzanne's words, *"definitely over."*

And, after the twelve-year period, they were drawn together again. By that point Suzanne had become involved in her spiritual path. She was opening psychically and learning about reincarnation; she wondered if she and Morgan had been together in a past life. His traditional religious training firmly intact, Morgan did not accept her newfound beliefs. *"What is your explanation for why we are together?"* she challenged him...to which he could only reply, *"Damned if I know!"*

When does an affair stop being an affair? The "impossible relationship" has lasted over thirty-five years—a commitment by any standards. Most of the time, their friendship has been painful to both of them. They did not want to hurt their families; keeping their relationship a secret held priority.

In her search to understand more about herself and, in Morgan's words, *"this illicit, immoral relationship,"* Suzanne obtained the assistance of an astrologer.

> *The astrologer looked at our charts and said "Suzanne, I've done a lot of relationship charts, and I've never found two that are closer than these. I have people all the time say, 'I love him so much, we must have been together before, we must be soul mates' and I search and search thinking, she says she loves him so much...it must be here someplace. But with your charts, I didn't even have to look; it jumps out all over."*

And months later, when Suzanne went to a channel*, a discarnate entity spoke from the Akashic** records:

THE ONE YOU NOW CALL MORGAN NEEDS TO
TAKE CARE OF YOU IN THE SENSE THAT HE NEEDS,

---

*A person who taps into the unconscious of the psyche or a discarnate entity.
**Universal memory banks and library of all thought and experience.

FOR HIS OWN GROWTH, TO KNOW THAT YOU ARE
WELL. IT IS NOT SOMETHING HE IS TO RISE ABOVE, IT
IS SOMETHING HE IS TO EXPERIENCE. THROUGH
ETERNITY YOU HAVE PLAYED WITH THIS SOUL. THIS
IS A SOUL DEDICATED — DEDICATED — TO THE
GROWTH OF FEELINGWITH YOU.
    THE PARTNERSHIP IS COMPLEMENTARY—WHILE
YOU DO THIS FOR ME, I DO THIS FOR YOU.
    WHAT PULLS YOU TOGETHER IS LOVE THAT
TRANSCENDS THE OUTER PERSONALITY OF THIS
LIFETIME. THE BOND IS ALWAYS...YOU CANNOT BREAK
IT, CHANGE IT. WHAT IS TO BE DONE IS JUST
LOVE—GROWING TO UNITY.
    IN THE SENSE THAT WE SPEAK OF KARMA ON THE
EARTH PLANE, THAT IS RESOLVED. AS YOU CHANGE, HE
CHANGES. THE OUTER PERSONALITIES CLASH BECAUSE
YOU ARE CONSTANTLY ADJUSTING TO EACH OTHER. AS
YOU CHANGE HE HAS TO CHANGE, SO YOU CLASH...AS
HE CHANGES, YOU HAVE TO CHANGE. YOUR SOULS ARE
EACH A PART OF THE OTHER IN GROWTH TO UNITY, SO
THAT YOU CONTINUE TO MEET, CONTINUE ALWAYS TO
AFFECT EACH OTHER.
    I DON'T EVEN THINK YOU CAN FEEL IT AS SUCH, BUT
HE IS ABSOLUTELY ESSENTIAL TO YOUR SUPPORT ON
EARTH. THAT DOES NOT MEAN THAT YOU HAVE TO BE
WITH HIM. YOU ARE AS ESSENTIAL TO HIM ON THE
EARTH AS HE IS TO YOU. I DON'T KNOW WHAT IT
IS...BUT THE BONDING...THE BONDING IS DONE.

Suzanne told us that the Akashic reading had a very
sobering effect on her. She convinced herself that she was
fine, and went to bed and drifted off to sleep.

*I don't remember crying in my sleep, but when I
woke up in the morning, my face was drenched with*

tears...and I felt as if my Soul—the deepest part of my Being—had grieved all night.

More months passed; she was assisted by another channel, at which time a different entity told her:

THE GOAL OF RELATIONSHIPS IS ONLY ONE: TO GIVE YOU WHAT YOU NEED ON YOUR WAY TO RETURN TO *ONE*. SOME NEED STRUGGLE, SOME NEED TO CLING, SOME NEED LONG-ENDURING RELATIONSHIPS, SOME TAKE ONE SHORT LESSON FROM A SOUL AND MOVE ON. SOME NEED TO LEARN WHAT "FOREVER LOVE" IS AND ISN'T.

WHEN ALL LESSONS ARE GATHERED, THEN—ONLY THEN IS IT POSSIBLE TO MARRY IN OUR VIEW. MARRY IS UNITE AT THE SOUL LEVEL. THAT KNOWLEDGE HAS BEEN TAKEN AND BASTARDIZED INTO WHAT HUMANS CALL MARRIAGE.

SECURITY, COMFORT, LOVE-ALWAYS ACTUALLY ONLY COMES WITH THE SOUL UNION. THE SOUL UNION MUST BE MADE ON THE PHYSICAL PLANE FOR HUMANS; THE BODY MUST BE INVOLVED. SOUL UNION DOES NOT NECESSARILY MEAN YOU GIVE UP YOUR BODY NEXT TIME. I SPEAK TO ONE WHO HAS DONE IT AND KNOWS.

Suzanne's mind was racing (Me? A Soul Union? Could it be with my husband?) when the channel said, "ARE YOU GOING TO ASK?" Suzanne replied, *"Will I get an answer?"* "YES." *"With whom?"* "WITH THE ONE YOU CALL MORGAN."

I was shocked—absolutely shocked...while another part of me knew I was hearing truth.

The information continued:

> ...MANY LIFETIMES AGO. HOW ELSE WOULD YOU
> KNOW? YOU HAVE DONE IT. LOVE IS EMOTION. IF GRIEF
> STANDS IN THE WAY, IT MUST BE RELEASED. YOUR
> DRIVE IS FREEDOM TO NOT CLOUD THE ABILITY GAINED
> UNTIL THIS TIME. YOUR SOCIETY TEACHES THERE IS NO
> FREEDOM IN MARRIAGE.
>   WHAT USUALLY HAPPENS IS THE SOUL BOND WILL
> OCCUR WITH ONE FIRST, LATER WITH MORE...FIND LIKE
> VIBRATION, LIKE CONSCIOUSNESS, AND LOVE. THERE
> CAN BE STRONG BONDS FROM THE OTHER CENTERS.
> THE SOUL UNION IS AT THE HEART CENTER—ONLY
> WHEN THE CENTERS BELOW ARE UNBLOCKED.

We have seen people who felt blocked mentally and/or emotionally; someone does body work and says, "Your chakras are clear, aligned, your energy is balanced." With such a pronouncement it sounds as if she is an Ascended Master! And yet the person remains blocked because beliefs, habits, desires, etc. have not changed. Bodywork unto itself may be an aid, but does not change consciousness.

Blockages in consciousness manifest on all levels or layers. The primary and most effective form of release is achieved through living as fully as one can in the emotional, mental and physical levels of being. Alignment of chakras and movement of energies in body work techniques, hypnotherapy, and all forms of holistic healing can be valuable aids in releasing blockages; however, they can only be just that—aids. The primary movement and release (willingness and effort) must come from the person himself and there is no substitute for the living experience. The channeled message to Suzanne continued:

WHEN YOU MAKE LOVE PHYSICALLY, YOU OPEN TO THE PARTNER AND ALL THE VIBRATIONS OF LOVE. WHEN YOU ARE UNBLOCKED IT IS POSSIBLE TO PULL IN MORE LOVE THAN YOU CAN HOLD. TAKING IN OF MORE IS TO PUSH OUT TOGETHER. WHEN THE HEART IS FILLED, THE SOUL PUSHES OUT AND THEY MERGE. IT HAPPENS, IT IS NORMAL, NORMAL TO TAKE THE STEPS TO ONE. YOUR SOCIETY EXCLUDES RELATIONSHIPS SO THE VIBRATION YOU SEEK IS NEVER FOUND.

Suzanne's mind went to Morgan's words many years previously: *"I want us to be One again."* Was he speaking out of the memory in his unconscious mind?

More months passed before Suzanne had the opportunity to question a third entity through a channel:

Is it true that I have a soul bond—a Soul Union—with Morgan?" "YES." *"Please tell me more about it.*

THE SOUL UNION GOES BACK INTO AN EARLY EGYPTIAN PERIOD—THE EARLY KINGDOMS BEFORE SOME OF THE PYRAMIDS. SOUL BONDING TO UNITY OCCURS WHEN THE CONSCIOUSNESS IN RELATIONSHIP IS RIGHT, AND WHEN THERE IS ENOUGH TIME, WHEN THE LOVING IS STRONG AND REPEATED. IT IS THE PROCESS OF BUILDING A SOUL-BRIDGE. IF THERE COULD BE ATOMS OF THE SOUL, YOU ARE EXCHANGING ATOMS OF THE SOUL. IT IS MORE OF AN EXCHANGE THAN CREATING A BABY, MORE, BECAUSE IT BECOMES A POOL—A COMMON POOL—OF SHARING. YOU LITERALLY HAVE ATOMS, IF THERE COULD BE ATOMS, OF MORGAN'S SOUL—HE OF YOURS.

What does that translate to today? How does that affect us today?

THE ATTRACTION THAT YOU FEEL FOR HIM AND HE
FOR YOU; THE CARING AND LOVING YOU GIVE EACH
OTHER DESPITE THE DIFFERENCES IN PERSONALITY;
THE SUPPORT. BEFORE YOU RETURNED IN THIS LIFE, IN
ADDITION TO THE SOUL UNION, YOU MADE A PROMISE
THAT YOU WOULD BE THERE FOR EACH OTHER.

Suzanne was told how rare it is for souls to reach the
state of consciousness and love to unite with another at
that level. In addition to the two individuals involved, the
state of consciousness on the planet at the time of
incarnation is also a factor. There are not many souls on
earth today (Suzanne was told it is less than ten percent)
who have experienced the Soul Union.

*I understand so much now. Our spirits support
each other so that it gives us strength to do what we
have to do in this life. It is why we have been able to
have a continuing relationship against all odds...yet
never made demands upon each other in any way. We
walk in different worlds. He is a conservative business
man dealing with corporate America. I work in a
holistic health environment.*

*Even though he does not accept reincarnation or
any of my beliefs, it is as if his soul understands what
my path is...and I understand what his path must be.
We are both still married to other people, and it's
okay, as it always has been. I hope some day Morgan
will have the peace that I have found through this
information from several sources. (I could never have
accepted it if it came through me or through only one
person.)*

*He still believes his religious teaching that he is
going to go to hell. No penance the church would give
could match the personal suffering he has lived with
all these years. All I can do is ask that his soul
continue to guide him along the path he needs to
follow and pray that he can grow beyond his rigid*

*programming in this life and remember who he is.
How sad that the personality of such a powerful soul
believes that he is going to hell for loving someone so
deeply.*

In the abyss of life my love longs.
Searching and believing in a place it belongs.
To gaze upon the face of love's heart,
to pass through the window of love's soul.

His love he keeps safe, secure...alone.
In solitude he longs to regain his throne.

My love is his, given with the freedom of wind.
He sees it, with a child's shyness, touches it.
Inconsistent, reluctant, closer he comes...
playing, basking in the glow of love.

With fear he bolts...bolts to safety for shelter
in his heart...remembering.
Alone and cold he grows;
denying the nurturing love of life.

My love waits,
what else can it do?...to him it belongs.
Given before love knew but to love.

THE ONLY TRUE MARRIAGE IS THE MARRIAGE OF THE SOUL

There is an absolute uniqueness to the Soul Union—it seldom occurs. Morgan and Suzanne could not achieve such a level of union in this life because of their blockages. The earth was in a different place when their original bond occurred thousands of years ago. The end of that life as well as other earth incarnations have limited their free spirits and put fear and guilt around their love.

A Soul Union can take place only with two people who are in a similar place in consciousness. Only then are they able to connect at every level of consciousness:

~ spiritually
~ with expression of that love equally felt
~ at a heart level—fully open to each other
~ giving and receiving energy (power) freely
~ in physical enjoyment of each other sexually
~ with a complete sense of safety and security

While making love, both people are receptive to the love-energy (God-Energy) between them. As they allow more openness into their auras and Being, the power, felt as passion, increases to the point of total orgasm. Total orgasm includes every chakra and energy system of the entire body. At that point there is an energetic joining of the souls. The only true marriage is the marriage of the souls.

"How To"
There are no breathing techniques
~ or positions
~ or foreplay
~ or holding of sexual energy
~ or a particular practice

When the consciousness is ready between two people, this joining of souls is automatic. There is no plan, no decision—only the full expression of love.

Why can't we do it? The answer is obvious—we are not free. We are not whole. We are limited and inhibited by the negative programming of our society that says, "Don't love." We are fear-based...living in fear of our ourselves and others. We do not have "open hearts." Until we can begin to move away from fear, we cannot love.

We seek love in/from another and are then disappointed when she does not live up to our unrealistic expectations. We project our image onto the other person and are shocked when she is not our image. We NEED and do not realize that the need first must be satisfied from within. Only that way can we become more whole—and only a whole person can unite with another in a Soul Union.

Unity is the first step in moving back to the God-Force. Greater soul bonding is not something we decide to do. It is something to move toward, recognizing that we can strive for greater love. We can go beyond the love depicted in movies and television. With the present state of consciousness on earth today, Soul Union at this level is almost impossible. Yet, as consciousness shifts, know that there really is a greater love—and if we work on ourselves, we can grow toward that.

We continue to expand and evolve by learning about love. The universe is ever expanding; we are part of that movement. The expansion of the soul is achieved through greater contact and experience in loving relationships. If we grow in the physical body and physical world to allow more love, when we pass into spirit we have filled ourselves with loving energy—the soul has expanded. Increase your capacity to love; we can do that only through the vehicle of other souls—not through intellect, academic degrees or hard work.

Because we are so often governed by fear, we worry that if we have a strong bond with someone, we cannot bond with another. We do not lose a spiritual bond; we do not lose the energy that is shared. It is important to realize that everyone offers something different. To expand, we have to experience more and we cannot receive all that we can with one soul and one life experience. We do not live our lives having only one experience.

BREAKING DOWN STRUCTURES

As more feminine energy comes into the earth to balance the patriarchal systems that have existed for thousands of years, we will see the breaking down of structures such as:

~ political institutions
~ religious institutions
~ educational institutions
~ military institutions
~ the institution of marriage

When we lift in consciousness to the true Divine spirit in us, we move beyond the need for a religious structure. When we lift in consciousness to responsibility in love, we move beyond the need for rules and regulations.

Our soul does not know structure in love. LOVE IS FREE-FLOWING ENERGY. AS SOON AS WE TRY TO STRUCTURE IT, WE LIMIT ITS VERY NATURE.

Traditional structured relationships fit only a percentage of people and leave out interracial, homosexual, differing ages, religions and cultures.

91

NOTHING IS WRONG BETWEEN CONSENTING ADULTS UNLESS THERE IS NO LOVE SHARED!

Love can exist and survive in the unconventional. Samantha told us she had two husbands. In reality, she was married to one man, who was approximately 10 years older, and in an intimate relationship with a man approximately 20 years younger than she. The younger man, Hans, was from another country and lived with Samantha, her husband and children for many years. Samantha's husband knew of the affair which lasted for approximately 16 years. Samantha loved both men and the only real conflict that she expressed was thinking she needed to let go of Hans so that he could find someone else, get married and have children. For Hans, however, he only wanted to be with Samantha. Samantha's only concern was resolved by her death; she was killed suddenly in an automobile crash.

It is important that we not judge another's soul's journey, or think we know what someone else's life lessons may be. The only thing we can be sure of is that with all affairs of the heart, a lesson of love is at the core.

Only the strongest soul mates can provide the biggest push. That does not mean our experience is going to be pleasant. The degree of difficulty is based upon our fear and rigidity. Very often the growth experience can be wrenching—heart, soul, body, being—to pull us out of a place where we would not otherwise go. The person who will force our growth is not going to be someone who is casual, just floating through our life—chances are we can let them go out as easily as they came. This person needs to be someone who touches every corner of our Being.

Suzanne knows that only she could have pushed Morgan to break his vows, and only he could have jolted her out of hers. Notice the word, vows—what a foreign concept to the soul. The soul does not make vows, the soul lives love. It is the human experience that sets up vows—structures that box us. This is how many live—it is real for the physical experience. When we set up the box, we get to break out of the box. Once we evolve, we will not need the body—it is as if we break out of the need for the body, too; in a sense, the body is a box. Anyone who has allowed intimacy with their soul mate has experienced the frustration of "I still can't get close enough to this person." The body gets in the way. It is the body that we want to get close to, and closeness to the body is still not close enough. The body that we want to get close to gets between us.

As there have been ebbs and flows in societal advancement, we have at times been much freer and less free. At this point in evolution, the consciousness is not high enough to handle a lack of structure. Without rules and regulations there would be chaos. Everyone seeks love and needs to find love. However, at this time we are probably not responsible enough to handle loving relationships in freedom. We have a potential to be infinitely freer in the body than we are now, but for the most part, society is not advanced enough for such freedom at this time.

If we really are talking about love, we are talking about RESPONSIBLE LOVE. If we have children, we are responsible for caring for those children. Ironically, with all of today's rules, many people are not responsible. If we do not move by changing structures, those structures fall. Occasionally a structure can be fluid enough for changes to occur (restructure). The same concept is true in business, nation, society, or an individual. When people will not change with life circumstances that require change, there will be a break in some manner.

As we continue to move toward fewer conditions around what love can be, love becomes freer. If we believe that love can be received from only one, receiving love depends upon: (1) our openness to her; (2) how able she is to give love. And if she cannot give the love that we need, are we going to deny ourselves love? Structure says the mate gives all the love. Within the structure of our society there are internal and external consequences—all coming out of limitation.

Understand, we are not encouraging irresponsible sex or mass orgies...we are talking about LOVE RESPONSIBILITY and the freedom of what love energy is. In times of increased disease potential through sexual contact, we must be responsible to our own body and that of our partner. We need to respect our body, energy, and spirit so that we share intimacy **only** with those partners who can respond in like vibration. And...to open ourselves to **receive**, we must respect and value that person's being/energy to **accept** it into our own. If we cannot do this in our current relationship, we must honestly ask, "Why am I in this relationship?"

We cannot promise that we will be committed to only one person. How can we make the best long-term decision for us and another person for the rest of our life? We do not usually know what is best for us tomorrow. We do not know what changes life will bring or what our greater soul need is.

When a love relationship ends suddenly and unexpectedly, it can create an explosion of passion when the souls meet again. Natalie met Stan in a costume shop. Both were seeking outfits to wear to Halloween parties. When she tried on a World War I nurse's outfit, Stan's entire psyche reacted; he recognized her as his love from another time. Natalie and Stan, both married to other people, began an affair. Natalie began to have spontaneous flashbacks of being with Stan in France during the war.

After a regression to that lifetime, Natalie questioned its reality, saying, "But I already saw all those memories." What she had *not* experienced in the flashbacks, however, was the stored emotion. She sobbed and sobbed at the sudden ending of her life. As her spirit left her body in the hospital setting, she cried out "No! I'm not ready to leave! Stan and I are going to be married...all our dreams...No! I don't want to go!"

Two days later, Stan called, saying he listened to the tape recording of the session. Knowing Natalie's hesitation about the session we were curious to know his reaction. "I know it's true!" he exclaimed.

Stan had his own regression to the same lifetime, confirming Natalie's memories. At her bedside, his grief over her death was uncontrollable. The regression continued, as we learned about Stan's life after Natalie's passing.

Although it was their initial intention to continue the affair and not break up their marriages, two years later Stan and Natalie happily shared that they were planning a wedding, in the small church in France, which still exists—the church they planned to get married in a lifetime ago.

We often hear, "What about marriage and children? You have to make a commitment, a vow to promise you are going to be together." If we are truly in touch with our heart and inner self, a commitment to the person is infinitely more substantial and can be more long-term. We are not saying we cannot commit to someone— especially when there are children; there is great responsibility involved. But to tie ourselves to a commitment simply for commitment's sake is limiting; it is not done in love.

Many of us are aware of married couples who have lived with a lack of love in the home — married fifty years, yet they made each other miserable. That lack of harmony in a home cannot help but trickle down to the children and grandchildren and affect them. If we stay in a marriage "for the sake of the children," we may not provide the best loving space. Assuming that is the position we take, after the children are grown and have left home will we stay together another thirty years? It is often fear that keeps us stuck. We are not too old to change as long as we are still breathing!

People deteriorate mentally and emotionally because they stop nurturing themselves. The concepts of love that we are talking about are those that stretch us beyond our limitations. It is about growth, it is about evolution. Growth and evolution do not come out of commitments, the boxes that we put ourselves in, and are bound and determined to stay in, even if everything in us is screaming to get out. "Oh no, because I made this promise." WE CANNOT PROMISE THAT WE WILL NEVER LOVE AGAIN...AND WHY WOULD WE WANT TO MAKE THAT PROMISE?!

If we incarnate intending to work on the issue of commitment, it may be a difficult lesson to learn. And yet, how do we move beyond that lesson? As with all growth, we stretch beyond our current boundaries. Commitment does not mean that we stay in commitment when there is not love involved.

We are aware that there is a radical perspective in what we are saying. The bottom line is that we have an obligation to love. COMMITMENT WITHOUT FREEDOM IS STRUCTURE—AND THAT IS CONFINING. We need, on an individual and societal basis to revamp that. According to marital and family psychotherapist, Murray S. Fleischer, Ph.D.:[*]

> There are approximately two hundred cultural societies in the world, and only four of them are monogamous, the rest are polygamous. In terms of the soul, I think marriage is an archaic institution and hasn't been modernized to handle what we do in the 1990's. There are so many people who are having more than one relationship; there are people who have written about it in terms of compartmentalization, in terms of not using the words "extra marital affair," which is also a very poor label.

A change is starting—this change is indicative of where society is and why marriage often does not work as it did in the past. Some worry that family values have fallen and everything is crumbling...yet perhaps we are expanding our concepts of family. If and when we can live in loving, responsible relationships, we create the strongest family that can exist, no matter how we grow and change. Our needs are greater than the structures that are imposed upon us. We are encouraging freedom in love and—RESPONSIBILITY TO OUR SPIRITUAL BEING!

Imagine how powerful a love relationship could be with someone with whom we can connect on **every** level:

~ Mentally - communicate with each other on an equal basis with challenges, understanding and acceptance.

---

[*]Used with permission.

~ Emotionally - allowing the freedom of each other's emotions, accepting their honesty and encouraging their expression.

~ Spiritually - recognizing the quality soul level of the other person and being able to communicate through the spirit.

~ Physically - expressing love in the physical world through our bodies, abilities and actions.

HEALING SOUL MATE RELATIONSHIPS

It is the nature of the soul to want to give and receive love. But human beings often limit the exchange of love to the idea of intense passionate physical interaction, and as soon as the intensity level changes we feel that we no longer have love. When the relationship intensity lessens, we may tend to shut the other person out. We are hurt and often turn inward emotionally. If we want the potential for a long-term relationship, which may have rocky periods and even periods of separation, we cannot shut down. Yes, we may need healing time, but as long as we are honest with ourselves and the other person, we will not shut out the love energy.

If we have a greater emotional need, we must be open to someone who can meet that need. It does not mean we have to discard another person. When Matthew drew William into his life, it was clear that William was more able than Kevin to meet Matthew's emotional need. The relationship between Matthew and William has evolved; so has the relationship between Matthew and Kevin, because the expectations on Matthew's part are not as demanding. Evolution of relationships is a process, a process that will continue, assuming it is allowed to occur.

For one human being to love another human being; that is perhaps the most difficult task that has been entrusted to us, the ultimate task, the final test and proof, the work for which all other work is merely preparation.

~Jeffrey Ryan*

Growth will not happen if we shut the person out of our heart. If two souls need the experience of being together and they are not given that opportunity, we may set up probabilities for a future life. We would meet the same person and again the opportunity for relationship would present itself...unless again we decline that opportunity. Denying love potential is like putting off work, "I'll do it tomorrow," and if we do not do it, the work continues to build.

So often we hear clients say, "I want a relationship, I want my life to change, I want someone in my life," so they go out to bars, to church, or social functions, to meet people. When we work on ourselves internally, we change our vibration. When we are at a point of readiness, we will draw someone who fits that new vibration. If we do not have a relationship now, perhaps a relationship with ourselves is what is needed. When the time is right and we are internally ready, we will draw a relationship—it may be one to teach, it may be one of challenge and/or passion, or comfort—all are of value. It is as if the unconscious, like a magnet, draws to it or repels, based upon what the deeper wisdom dictates. If a decision is made on the unconscious level, the personality consciousness cannot indefinitely override it.

*Used with permission.

A client who has a strong unconscious belief in pain and suffering will inevitably attract a relationship which will provide that. It may be a soul mate who plays that role. In another example, Suzanne held a belief that "love is loss" because again and again Morgan and Suzanne had lived past lives where he left her and then she left him. After years of internal work, she changed her belief system to recognize that "We may not be together physically, but the love is not lost—the love exists."

Matthew firmly believed in "One and only." That attitude comes out of a belief that it has to be one person...or one person in a monogamous relationship for the rest of our lives. Indeed if we truly find love, it will be forever...but in the physical dimension things change all the time; we need those challenges to evolve spiritually. For Matthew, because he so adamantly believed in that One Love, it was more difficult for him to move toward another relationship after the breakup. His belief changed after internal work that effected the external; he drew William into his life. The process does work. Reframing belief systems internally may take years, but it does work.

Ed is now in an exclusive relationship with another woman, yet the love between him and June is still very real. Factors in their relating to each other have changed somewhat, but there is no doubt on the part of either of them that the love exists. Even in this example, of a couple who was married for over 33 years and separated, the love still exists. Any new mates will, instead of fostering avoidance and negativity—often the norm in such matters—need to accept that the love between Ed and June remains.

Although each type of soul bond and connection brings a unique experience, the ultimate purpose of that experience is the same—to bring us to greater love.

Spirit is forever—love is forever. In the body, physical love forever cannot exist. There is a definite termination to the physical life. Fear of that termination creates a lack of trust of the love—the person will die or leave for another, so we stop trusting the love.

In the case of Carol and Peter, they had only two and one-half years together. He is gone, as far as the physical dimension is concerned. And yet, the spiritual bond that they share remains.

After a deep loss, it is not easy to open our hearts again. Healing soul mate relationships does not always mean detaching or walking away. Matthew will always love Kevin, but he will not keep pouring energy or emotion into a situation that is not receptive or reciprocal—not when giving is not in his best interest or is not loving to himself. This does not mean we stop loving the other person; sometimes all we can do is be receptive to that love. It certainly does not mean that we allow an abusive relationship into our life.

By recognizing that we deserve more self love, we lift in consciousness and move away from the limitations of past-life issues. In a situation where we feel as if we are suffering, we have the potential to make change. The following ways move us through issues:

~   Remember (consciously). Go to the source of it, such as in a regression, to release and reprogram.
~   Go through the experience (unconsciously). Live the situation.

Once a relationship ends and we can allow another love into our life, internal change has occurred. We are speaking of practical applications with proven results; real changes can be made. These are not just ethereal concepts.

Soul mate relationships do not necessarily manifest

as the happy, romantic, ideal situations that we tend to envision. If we bring a soul mate relationship into our life, our goal is to expand love—which does not necessarily mean that it is going to end happily ever after.

We need to find internal healing and peace regarding the relationship. This kind of healing is self healing/love; we cannot be responsible for where the other person is with the situation. If the other person is not ready to heal, we can still heal. When we think of healing, we may picture an active, healthy relationship with the other person, but true healing does not necessarily mean that. Internally where are you with it? When you think of the other person, when that person's name comes up, do you cringe inside, do you hurt inside? If so, chances are that you are still in the process.

It is nice if healing can be done mutually, and a comfortable place can be found, but this is not always the case because someone else is involved. If we let him determine our action, non-resolution could continue on for several more lifetimes. And if you recognize that it is time to heal, then this is an opportunity for growth which comes with releasing attachment and expectations.

The reason that the relationship between Morgan and Suzanne has endured through time and adverse circumstances is that the love bond is so strong and the two members of that relationship, consciously or not, know that a spiritual connection is there. Although their personalities didn't have all the answers, they were willing to cooperate with the process.

Because they share a spiritual bond, Morgan and Suzanne have been able to give incredible freedom to each other and not make demands in the physical dimension. So often, one person threatens the other: "If you do..., I'm out of here," or "If you go with this person, you'll never hear from me again." This kind of attitude is in contrast to the love.

Because Morgan and Suzanne's physical needs were met in other ways, they could allow each other that freedom, yet this obviously is not the norm or a typical situation. Many people do act out of hunger and from not having needs fulfilled. But if the bond is real, situations such as lack of contact, presence of another lover, or living five hundred miles apart do not threaten the bond.

For a relationship to be healthy, it is important to maintain an honest movement of energy. We view honesty as verbal expression, and this is true. However, it is also important to be honest in **feelings** and in their expression. This is the only way to maintain vitality in a relationship. Honesty is integral to a healthy relationship. DISHONESTY EQUATES TO DETERIORATION IN RELATIONSHIPS.

If I am upset with you, ideally you are the one to whom I should speak, and vice versa. If we move the energy by talking to the other person, this talking improves our relationship, in the sense that we are not adding resentment or blockage. When we discuss something, we take power away from negative build-up, and re-channel the energy back to a flowing, communicating situation.

Healing soul mate relationships means filling ourselves with loving energy. If we have not been filled with loving energy, we cannot provide that same loving energy to another person.

In order to have true communication, not only do we need to be honest in our expression with the other person, but we need to take responsibility for our own feelings. Blame is not an appropriate response in a healthy relationship. We give power to negative feelings when we feed them—"I'll show him." And that is what happens when a couple, who once stood together at the altar end up bickering over who is going to get the coffee table in the divorce. Knock-down, drag-out fights about things—the table, the china, etc. are not really over those things; the real issue cannot be dealt with honestly, so inanimate objects become the focus.

We live with ourselves—our own Being. We can never get away from ourselves. Are we going to live with this person who is constantly in negative thoughts and feelings? Or are we going to create a Being who is in a space of more loving energy. Many people seem to come from a perspective of "we can't change ourselves" ...but they do not hesitate to try to change someone else. We tend to focus outside ourselves. **We can change only ourselves, we can never change another person.**

Although we have been encouraging freedom in love throughout this book, it is not as simple as saying, "This isn't pure love, I'm getting out." If a particular choice is a soul decision, we are not going to avoid it. The personality is not strong enough to override the soul—not for any length of time. If the soul is pushing, the soul is relentless; it has nothing but time. The personality has a very timed life.

Inside, we know—listen! There are situations where a person continues to give and give and we have to respect that, if she feels strongly about her choice to give. For whatever reason (fulfilling karma or moving through a blockage) giving is what she needs to do. Our personalities cannot fully grasp the greater wisdom of the soul.

In retrospect Matthew now realizes that Kevin was giving love. That kind of giving may not have been Matthew's way, it may not have been what he would like to have received, but Kevin was giving. Matthew could not receive that love because he was so caught up in his expectations. The truth of the matter is that Kevin was expressing loving energy, and Matthew was not able to fully receive it. Expectation restricts one's ability to receive love.

ENDINGS AND EVOLUTION

Change comes through evolution, and evolution comes through change. It is a gradual process affected by our physical environment and the energy of our attitudes and spiritual essence.

Life is evolution—which occurs very slowly and is determined by the needs and qualities in a being and/or situation. As surely as evolution occurs in the physical, it happens on every other level as well. It is theorized that eventually we will no longer need our little toes; as their usefulness diminishes, so will their presence on our bodies. We evolve and let go of those things we no longer need.

As mass consciousness moves to greater awareness, change/evolution occurs, though we never really know where we are headed. There may not be a set place to go. The direction of evolution is affected by our input. Like our environment, our spiritual evolution is ever changing and responsive to what it receives. With constant direction and guidance toward higher love vibration, evolution of the spirit occurs. If we desire evolvement to higher love, then that is what must be nurtured and encouraged.

When a relationship ends, the energy between the people has already turned away. Likely the energy change began years before the physical reality of parting happens.

The karma has been completed...or the soul has new lessons to learn...new growth is taking place. Then why is letting go so hard?! Change—the unknown—fear. The old relationship is safe, comfortable, and known.

When a vibrational change occurs between people, that change means that at least one has grown—thoughts, experiences, feelings, beliefs have changed within the Being—he is no longer the same person.

Separation or divorce need not be the failure that is too often felt by a couple. And...the understanding of vibrational change can contribute to supporting each other through difficult days involved in separating physically.

It becomes difficult when the lines are so hard to see: How do we determine when a relationship is not good for us and we should leave...or if we need to stay to face things within ourselves. If we remove confrontation or adversity in life, we may be removing potential for growth, as well as lowering the potential for passion, excitement, enthusiasm and joy. If we are afraid of pain and anger in what we see as negative emotions, we are also limiting more love, more joy, greater feelings. We suffer fear that we might lose the joy—fear that we cannot trust the other person always to be there for us. The truth is, we cannot. But unless we can acknowledge that truth and live in the love of the present moment, we will pull back from feeling.

Sometimes a couple is separated physically, but their energies (or the energy of one connected to the other) remain intact. Thoughts and emotional ties to the person will keep energy connected. Anger, as well, connects us through energy. Whether we are talking about a divorce (or even expressing anger at deceased parents), the emotional vibration of anger will keep us tied—not free. When a relationship ends, the energy connection may not end. If one holds on, that energy is one-sided...the cord still exists with one, even though it is no longer generated from the other person. When there is a break on the physical level, that break is felt strongly. The spiritual connection may still exist. The psychic connection can be experienced and felt through an energy path, similar to a phone line, depending on how receptive the two people are.

In a triangle (a common scenario), the one who is left alone is often angry and hurt. Every time she thinks of the former mate she feels pain, sadness or anger. Healing does not necessarily mean that two people will be back together again. Reuniting is always a possibility, but such an outcome is not inevitable nor should it even be the goal. Healing means being able to think about him in a loving way, but also allowing him to be where he is, knowing that he is where he needs to be.

We need to be honest with the way we feel, not viewing ourselves as victim. Isn't it great that you drew that person to you! YOUR soul brought him to you. Thinking of a situation in this light takes away the "Why me?!"

It is important to shatter the concept of victimhood and blame. It is hard for people to say..."I brought this on, but why." If we have determined that we need to suffer about something, we will not easily let it go. At a deep level we believe that we deserve our suffering or we need it for growth.

I would like to beg you to have patience with everything unresolved in your heart and try to love the questions themselves as if they were

locked rooms or books written in a very foreign
language. Don't search for the answers, which
could not be given to you now, because you
would not be able to live them. And the point
is to live everything. LIVE the questions now.
Perhaps then, someday far into the future,
you will gradually, without even noticing
it, live your way into the answer.

~Jeffrey Ryan*

An example of victimhood might be that of a woman whose husband is having an affair. She maintains the victim role by saying, "I was a good wife, I don't deserve this!" Wrong! If our mate has an affair, our soul has brought this experience to us so that we can learn from it. How will we handle this situation? If we blame, possess, threaten and manipulate while operating from a "Why me?" perspective—we may "save" the marriage, but pull him away from what his soul needs to experience. The husband needs something that she is not providing, which reflects the greater need for change in the relationship. To view this from a larger perspective, there is no blame, there are needs which are not being met. If we can look inside and recognize that we are not filling a need—we can then determine the step that is right for us.

A client says with the intellect, "If I have to do without him, I will," while her emotions and aura are screaming at being alone—utter fear! Being able to recognize that she can live alone shows movement. However, this recognition comes through the mental layer, which is easier to penetrate. The layer that she needs to employ is the emotional layer, but that layer is

---

*Used with permission.

heavier and more difficult to manage. It is imperative that emotions be expressed; if they are turned inward illness may result—illness in any form.

Healing begins with the Self. We draw to ourselves the energy that we need because we either cannot find it in ourselves or have not yet developed it. Once we build it in, we have no "need" for the person anymore. That does not mean that we discard them, it means that we can meet each other with more wholeness.

Allow yourself to be guided by the wisdom of the soul. Acts of love to the spirit can bring only freedom and enlightenment.

BALANCING SOUL ENERGY

Although the soul nature is androgynous it seems that in a splitting or separation of soul energy, we have taken on a primary quality of either masculine or feminine (yang/yin) matter. In movement through time, incarnations assist in building in the opposite matter in order to reach wholeness—androgyny once again.

As we have seen in our work, sometimes the outer personality is diametric to the inner being. For example, Suzanne has a strong mind/inner being that is quite evident, a projection of masculine energy. Her personality in this life is that of a very feminine woman. Her mannerisms, nature, interests and comfort level portray a woman who enjoys her femininity. Morgan's inner being is of a sensitive, emotional, nurturing nature. His outer personality is of powerful masculine energy—one of movement, accomplishment, a success oriented, building nature.

It appears that in order to attain balance, we build in through incarnations those qualities that are lacking, based upon the original separation.

Matthew's soft, flowing, receptive personality belies the intense, warrior energy of his soul. If others see only the outer personality, they see the qualities that Matthew is learning to build into his soul—they miss his true nature. Kevin's personality is outgoing, assertive and confident, while his inner being is gentle, sensitive and tender. Kevin is building masculine energy into his soul energy. If we consider these two people as twin souls, then when the original cell split occurred, the primary energy split may have effected an energy separation of masculine and feminine (yang/yin) energy.

Of course no one person is all yin or all yang. We all have masculine and feminine energy within our Being. Our language does not adequately represent the concepts that we are trying to share.

In building essence to balance soul energy, we move to the opposite quality—incorporating life experience assists in the building. The manifestation of a primary masculine/feminine tendency in the personality serves not only to provide balance, but also manifests in practical aspects of our lives. Morgan's masculine personality promotes a strong inclination and high success rate in business while Suzanne's feminine personality allows her to be well suited and successful in her private healing practice and served her as a loving, nurturing mother and wife.

Imbalance in our Beings results in undesirable qualities and experiences manifesting in our lives. One example of imbalance can be seen in sexual intimacy between lovers. To achieve a mutual, fully gratifying sexual experience of giving and receiving, both participants need to flow with their masculine AND feminine energy. Lack of balance affects all aspects of our lives—sexual intimacy, platonic interaction, nurturing, career—even our ability to simply enjoy life.

The greater freedom we can allow for love—lack of expectation—the greater level of love that love can attain. We must learn to not equate love with emotional attachment—LOVE IS EMOTIONAL CONNECTION, NOT ATTACHMENT. In fear we try to hold on, attach emotionally, thinking that we will lose the love bond if we let go, but in truth love can only strengthen in our connection when we stop attaching.

This same rule applies to all the layers of our consciousness. As love is emotional connection, in its highest form, it can be a physical, emotional, mental **and** spiritual connection.

Our souls long for this sense/feeling of connection, which explains our personal and societal belief in the ultimate and unending love experience. And, although it may indeed be our soul mates who are bringing us to this "perfect" love, they probably will not do it in the way or time that we hoped for it to be. Love by nature, like the soul, will always seek its highest form, and time is inapplicable. However, this growth can occur only through process, and trusting in and freely allowing this process is anything but easy. Ease is no more the goal than is pain. LOVE is the goal.

CONCLUSION

The purpose of our existence,
the purpose of our incarnations on the earth,
the purpose of our relationships,
is to become a more integrated part of the God-Energy.

ARE YOU LIVING FEAR...
OR ARE YOU LIVING LOVE?

Janet Cunningham, Ph.D., is owner of BREAKTHROUGHS TO THE UNCONSCIOUS® a private practice in Columbia, Maryland. She is an internationally known speaker, seminar leader, and Board Certified specialist in regression therapy who specializes in breaking through blockages in the unconscious mind. Janet is author of *A Tribe Returned* and *Inner Selves: The Feminine* Path to Weight Loss (*for men and women who value their intuitive nature.)*

"The blockages in your unconscious mind prevent you from being free—as surely as if your hands were tied with ropes."

®

Michael Ranucci is a personal fitness trainer. He is a sensitive specializing in perceiving energy patterns and hidden emotional imbalances. Michael is a poet who has written a series titled *Aquarelle* and *Expressions of Running Deer*, a portion of which is published in *A Tribe Returned*, the story of a group reincarnation experience. Michael resides in Naples, Florida.

*"We, as beings of God, on **all** levels are made up of God-stuff—love energy. The greater the freedom we allow ourselves, the greater the love that will flow into our lives."*